NIGERIA
More Years Eaten By the Locusts

George Ehusani

Adonis & Abbey Publishers Ltd

24 Old Queen Street,
London SW1H 9HP

Website: http://www.adonis-abbey.com
E-mail Address: editor@adonis-abbey.com

Nigeria:
39 Jimmy Carter Street,
Suites C3 – C6 J-Plus Plaza,
Asokoro, Abuja, Nigeria.
Tel: +234 (0) 7058078841/08052035034

British Library Cataloguing-in-Publication Data
A catalogue record for this book is available from the British Library

ISBN: 9781913976125

NIGERIA
More Years Eaten By the Locusts

George Ehusani

ADONIS & ABBEY
PUBLISHERS LTD

Table of Content

Chapter One
When God is Not to Blame

Chapter Two
Nigeria: The Struggle Continues

Chapter Three
Salisu Buhari as a Metaphor

Chapter Four
A Jubilee Year Prayer

Chapter Five
Nigeria: Neglect of the Common Good

Chapter Six
Transforming our Prisons to Correctional Centres

Chapter Seven
NIGER DELTA: Our Guilt and Shame

Chapter Eight
Where is our Sanity?

Acknowledgement

The process of putting together in book form this collection of articles, essays and public lectures, under the title, *More Years Eaten by the Locusts*, has been a rigorous one, involving the very painstaking work of sorting through hundreds of my writings, covering a period of twenty years, which were not originally filed away in any particular order or classified under any particular headings or themes. So, the task of sorting through the folders in my computer and identifying which articles and papers belong together, and how they could be appropriately classified under the broad title of this present publication was an enormous one.

It is therefore with immense gratitude that I acknowledge the very painstaking groundwork done on the raw articles and papers by Rex Emma Odoemenam over a period of nearly two years. Next is the very rigorous task of organising and re-organising the originally selected papers by my good friend Dr. Anthony Okeregbe of the University of Lagos. I am also grateful to Prof. Taiwo Abioye who took time to go through all the papers at this early stage and offered very useful advice on the way forward.

As the manuscript assumed some discernible shape, I must acknowledge the diligent editorial work carried out on it by my brother, Fr. Richard Ehusani, and the intense proof-reading work executed by the indomitable Greg Aiyemo, the Editor-in-Chief of Lux Terra Publications. I must also express my gratitude to Mike Egbe for typesetting the book, and to Prof. Jideofor Adibe of Adonis & Abbey Publishers, who organised the professional indexing of the book.

Above all, I give thanks and praise to our Almighty God who has revealed himself definitively in Christ Jesus, and whose civilisation of love inspired most of the articles, essays and reflection in this collection. May his name be praised forever.

George Ehusani

George Ehusani

Foreword

...after eight years of military dictatorship, the worst form of which was manifested in the Abacha dispensation, Nigerians had hoped for a period of peaceful transition to a just, equitable, democratic and peaceful society. We had hoped for a new Nigerian society where we can once again have the opportunity to channel our enormous national endowments to positive use for the advancement of our teeming population. We had hoped for a new Nigerian society where we can celebrate the richness of our diverse languages, cultures and religions. We had hoped for a new Nigerian society where we can take our rightful place in the comity of nations and compete in the advancement of science and technology. But rather than make progress in these directions, multiple crises and conflicts have plagued post-military Nigeria..." (George Ehusani, "Youth Restiveness, Social Instability and the Quest for Peace," December 11, 2003).

The foregoing passage can be taken as the thesis statement for this collection of essays on the Nigerian condition by Fr. George Ehusani, titled *"Nigeria: More Years Eaten by the Locust"*, a sequel to an earlier book with a similar title - *"Nigeria: Years Eaten by the Locust" (Kraft Books, 2002)* - a collection of essays on Nigeria's misfortune under military rule, specifically, the period between the annulment of the June 12, 1993 Presidential election and the military's eventual exit from power in May 1999. The June 12, 1993 Presidential election was legitimately adjudged to be the freest and the fairest election in Nigeria at that point in the country's history. Its annulment by the Ibrahim Babangida administration had far-reaching negative and embarrassing consequences for Nigeria, locally and internationally. Fr. George Ehusani, Deputy Secretary General of the Catholic Secretariat in Lagos, Nigeria, at the time, was a major witness to history. The Catholic Conference of Bishops had taken a principled stance against dictatorship and bad governance which was evidenced in the misconduct of the military elite, represented by the regime's determination to suppress the people's will, violate their rights and dignity and deny them the right and the power to choose and determine their own affairs. Nigeria under the Abacha regime was at best, a vast prison yard. No one was spared, not even the civil society.

The Catholic Church of Nigeria was indeed one of the principal voices of reason against tyranny in Nigeria. Fr. George Ehusani was in the right place at the right time. A poet, singer, writer, teacher, polemicist, he deployed his talents to speak truth to power and amplify the concerns of the Church about the impoverished, marginalized and abused people of Nigeria. It was during this period that he wrote a piece of much-needed and prescient book on the role of the Church in society: *A Prophetic Church (1996)*. A Prophetic Church in his definition is the Church of the poor, a Church that meets the people at the point of their needs and gives them hope, a Church that speaks truth to power from the pulpit, a crusading Church of Christ that espouses values and ideals and points to a higher level of reckoning and awareness beyond the quotidian, discouraging, debilitating, limiting forces of poverty, ignorance, disease and squalor that the poor have to deal with. Ehusani's idea of the Prophetic Church provides a sharp contrast, disturbing and instructive to the discerning as it may seem, to the rise in Nigeria at the same time of a stomach-driven brand of Christianity that appropriated, perhaps misappropriated, the values and ethos of a decadent society: a society driven by ostentation, greed and opportunism. The role of the religious establishment in Nigeria has always been a subject of curiousity and interrogation, and the Church of Christ has found itself on both sides of the spectrum: clerics of different faiths who dispense prayers to those who suppress the people, and a minority that uses their calling to promote peace, progress and stability. Ehusani stands on the latter side of the spectrum.

It would not be out of place to say that he and Fr. Matthew Hassan Kukah, whom he later succeeded, presided, one after the other, over the golden moments of the Catholic Secretariat in Nigeria's contemporary history. I remember also, Fr. John Uba Ofei, now of blessed memory. They organized conversations around the central issues of democracy, values and national progress. They actively engaged and mobilized the civil society. They formed alliances with other groups in civil society and turned the Catholic Secretariat into a platform for robust intellection and truth-telling. They wrote prolifically on the pages of newspapers. Ehusani also wrote newspaper editorials, in his capacity as a consultant/member of the Editorial Board of *The Guardian* newspaper for many years. His reference to the locust is an apt, compelling metaphor. A locust is a destructive animal, parasitic, gregarious, and disruptive. It tears down whatever is in its path. A threat. Ehusani's message is that the military were like locusts, but their civilian successors, since 1999, are not in any way different.

His famous response was an invocative and optimistic piece titled "Never Again." The piece bristles with hope about change and a new Nigeria and a brighter future ahead of the country. That eponymous essay can be found in the earlier book. But the question is: what has happened since the author raised the poser: Never Again! He provides the answer himself: the locusts have not stopped their acts of destruction. And why? In 1998/1999, the expectation was that the exit of the military and the emergence of a new dispensation in form of the return to civilian rule would automatically translate into change. It was thought that change in the mode of governance would necessarily guarantee good leadership, participatory democracy and a collective sense of ownership. In this book, Ehusani tells us that this has not happened. Nearly every chapter is an expression of frustration and angst. Nigeria is at a standstill. The locust remains resilient. Is Fr. Ehusani repeating his message: "Never Again?" Never again what? He too is somewhat perplexed. He may be disappointed, however, but he does not regret past struggles, he does not despair either, but he paints a haunting picture of the Nigerian dilemma and offers alternative ways of being - in the people's interest, the common good and how Nigeria can be transformed, reformed and rescued. What grips is the repetitiveness of the Nigerian problem, how both the military and the civilian are united in foisting a culture of failure on the country.

It really did not take long before Fr. Ehusani saw the future beyond the military. By July 25, 1998, he had observed in a piece titled "When God is not to Blame," the tendency of the average Nigerian to heap every blame on God. General Abdulsalami Abubakar, General Abacha's successor, under whose watch Chief M.K.O. Abiola died suddenly, on July 7, 1998, after four years in the military gulag, had said that the late democrat's death was an "act of God." Ehusani disagreed. He decried the tendency to blame God for human errors and omissions. A Catholic priest-writer defending God and condemning any effort to mischaracterize Him would be a natural expectation, except that the use of God as referent by this particular author is consistently backed with irrefutable evidence about the failure of man. Ehusani drew attention in Abiola's case to how the political leader was maltreated by the state: the acute malnourishment to which he was subjected, how he was denied access to good medical attention and physical exercise, his incarceration in a poorly ventilated and poorly lighted room, the injustice of it all. Like General Musa Yar'Adua before him, MKO Abiola died in detention. The author argues that God was not to blame. Moral evils cannot be attributed to God. Ehusani writes instructively: "the good Lord is not the author of evil and so cannot take responsibility for tragedies that are a direct acquiescence of the moral choices of free human agents." He warned as far back as 1998 that there were multiple layers of resentment in the Nigerian society which could result in a "crisis of monumental proportions" such as the world witnessed in Rwanda and Bosnia. That crisis is today upon the country!

Nigeria soon returned to civilian rule on May 29, 1999. The people were jubilant at the possibility and the reality also of a second liberation: the first in 1960 was from colonial overlords, the second in 1999, was seen as a liberation from internal colonialism. On June 7, 1999, Fr. George Ehusani announced in a piece of the same title that in "Nigeria: The Struggle Continues." He sounded a note of caution: "We may have won the battle, but we have certainly not won the war." He observed that Nigerians would be foolhardy to rely on the goodwill of the newly elected politicians, indeed that would be "the height of naivety." And so, he wanted civil society stakeholders to remain vigilant and stand firm as "watchmen for democracy and justice, watchmen for accountability and transparency, and watchmen for the responsible management of the economy and conduct of politics." The rest of the book provides ample evidence of how right Ehusani's hunches were. The many episodes of Nigeria's democratic experience that he comments upon cover the Obasanjo Presidency (1999 – 2007), but the same patterns, both inherited and new, persist into the post-Obasanjo Presidential era. If the military were insensitive, uncaring and rapacious, their civilian successors from 1999 forwards have been no different. The watchdogs didn't have to wait for too long before returning to the trenches, after what seemed like an initial spell of fatigue.

Indeed, the Fourth Republic began on a dramatic note with the scandal of Salisu Buhari, Speaker of the House of Representatives, whom Ehusani describes as "the first major casualty of the new dispensation in Nigeria." Within seven months, Salisu Buhari, the fourth person within the democratic hierarchy, had to resign as Speaker and Member of the House of Representatives. It was found that he lied about his age and educational qualifications. It is not just the shamelessness and visionlessness of the ruling elite that attracts Ehusani's attention, he writes also in this collection about the leadership crisis in the country, the combined forces of "corruption, greed, neglect and abuse," the marginalization of the weak, the defenseless and minorities in general, and a complete neglect of the common good. The author paints a canvas on which he deposits haunting images of the failure of the Nigerian elite in the post-military era to make democratic rule worthwhile for the people. There are echoes of the kind of disappointment we find on the pages of Ngugi wa Thiong'O's *This Time Tomorrow (1970)*, wherein the same characters who fought for Uhuru, that is independence, with high expectations are compelled to look back and wonder whether the struggle was meaningful in retrospect.

The pages of "More Years Eaten by the Locust" are in the same manner, filled with the author's account of tales of neglect and abuse: in the Niger Delta – Jesse, Odi, Egborode, Zaki Biam and elsewhere, the general loss of the African Humanistic Tradition, as seen in the spread of violence across the land, the promotion of a culture of hate, the menace of religious fundamentalism and extremism, the manipulation of religion – in this regard, the imposition of the Sharia as a legal orthodoxy in 12 states in the Northern part of the country, the persecution of Christians and the erosion of trust. Nigerian youths, as seen in this book, lack faith in their own country because they have been disappointed by the adult society, and hence they opt to become foot-soldiers for violence, war and the ethnic atomization of the Nigerian society. Ehusani writes about elite conspiracy, the moral degeneracy of the Nigeria Police and the failure of public institutions, indeed state failure and the reign of absurdity. Confronted with such a post-military rule Nigeria, hijacked by rogues and gangsters claiming to be professional politicians but for whom politics means the looting of the people's resources, conspiracy and opportunism, Ehusani bursts out in desperation: "Help! Maniacs are in power" (November 11, 2002). He asks: "Where is our sanity?" A pertinent question.

What is known is that most countries succeed because they have a critical elite, a class of leaders who are committed to the common good and who are willing to serve their people and make a difference, not politicians whose main goal is to "capture the state" for their own selfish reasons. After a visit to Canberra, Australia, May 2004, and the Haggai Institute, Singapore, October 2004, Ehusani writes that "It's Leadership, Stupid" (November 10, 2004). It is difficult to argue either with this conclusion or Ehusani's conviction that the Nigerian situation is not irredeemable. Nigerians may have made a mess of their country and its rich resources due to crass materialism and selfishness, corruption, and the politicization of the state but with visionary leadership, the same people can develop a sense of cohesion and re-build the country for the good of all. The author oscillates between prayers for the nation, analysis of problems and specific recommendations. But have we not seen and heard it all?

Clearly nations fail, or succeed, relative to the quality of leadership within the polity, but still, there isn't one formula that fits all cases, as seen in the many case studies in Buchir Sharma's *Break Out Nations: In Pursuit of the Next Economic Miracles (2012)*. But perhaps a common thread would be a determination to commit to national progress and transformation. Where is that critical elite in Nigeria today? Is Nigeria ready to break out of the chains of retrogression? Where are the Nigerians, the new citizens who can make the difference? The Nigerians at the border gates rushing to seek better fortunes in North America or anywhere else in the world? Or the disillusioned lot moaning and groaning at home under "a heavy yoke" imposed by a problematic elite that punishes them with both "whips and scorpions?"

Ehusani is both a student of history and its attentive critic. He wrote many of the essays in this book during major turning points in Nigerian history; the book is now being published at yet another season of a major transition in Nigeria: the lead up to the 2023 general elections. The same old arguments at the heart of the national question persist; the tunnel ahead remains as dark, and clogged with uncertainties to a degree higher than before. Nigeria keeps tottering on the brink; what holds it together perhaps is the people's individual heroism and resilience: the missing link is the deployment of all that energy on a collective scale, buoyed up by a shared vision of national greatness.

Fr. Ehusani preaches hope and points to possibilities. His inspiration is probably drawn from that famous passage in the Scriptures – Joel 2: 25 – 32:

> So I will restore to you the years that the swarming locust has eaten/The crawling locust/The consuming locust/And the chewing locust/ My great army which I sent among you/You shall eat in plenty and be satisfied/And praise the name of the Lord your God/ Who has dealt wondrously with you/And My people shall never be put to shame…

The bigger question for Nigeria is: When? Or better still - Quo Vadis? For how long will Nigeria continue to dance around on the same spot, tied down by the same divisive issues. There are no easy answers obviously, but all Nigerians have a responsibility to collectively wield pesticides to wage a mortal battle against the locust destroying the national farm, so that this country can fulfil its potentials and bloom. This book confronts us with hard truths about the Nigerian condition and the need to admit that all has not been well, with and without the military, and the starting point for reconstruction is an admission of the moral evils that plague us and the responsibility for it, not as a metaphysical construct but as the sum total of our collective omissions. This is a welcome contribution to the existing literature on the state of the Nigerian union.

Reuben Abati
Newspaper Columnist, Radio & Television Anchor,
former Chairman of the Editorial Board of the Guardian Newspaper,
and former Senior Special Assistant on Media Affairs
to President Goodluck Jonathan.

Preface

To the avid reader of Nigeria's social commentaries or the attentive listener to reflections on the country's spiral moral and material developmental decline, Father George Ehusani is no stranger. His pen constantly threatens to run dry and his voice go hoarse as he churns and belts out endlessly prophetic proclamations on the darkening horizon over Nigeria's socio-political and economic firmament.

He is truly in his element in this new publication of *Nigeria: More years eaten by the Locust*, a collection of some thirty-one chronologically-ordered articles spanning twenty years from 1998 to 2018. The precursor to this publication, *Nigeria: Years eaten by the Locust* covered his writings during the period that Nigeria was subjected to the dictatorial regime of General Sani Abacha (from 1993 to June 1998).

This new publication like the one before it, further exposes the protracted angst in the land, engendered by the serial despoliation and stunting of the country's immense natural endowments and development and potential, under the despotic rogue regimes of the military. Recognising the imperative of recorded history as an important tool for human development, Father Ehusani has put together the warning signals he had signposted along Nigeria's regressive track. Short of highlighting the destructive social impact of the invading locusts that have rendered the country truly desolate in an otherwise abundant environment, what else can a concerned social critic with no defining powers do to jar the conscience of the nation?

A major plank of the writer's commentaries is the quality of leadership that has bestrode this land over the past decades, a succession of clueless, self-serving elite opportunists that have entrenched themselves in the leadership space, with no intention to learn from history. The author's pain begs the question whether our leaders ever evaluate the outcome of their leadership enterprise for concrete indices of progressive nation building and national development; whether a landscape of blossoming corruption and insecurity befits a credible legacy; whether our place at the tail end of global classification of progress is acceptable and satisfactory.

The unrelenting episodes of degradation in virtually all fronts of wholesome human development exhaustively chronicled in these articles clearly show that the pestilence that has afflicted us over the years is very much alive. Like a broken record, *More years eaten by the Locust* plays the lamentations of a shipwreck floundering in the throes of drowning. The writer has enumerated in this volume as in the one before, issues that strike at the core of our common humanity – love, fellow feeling, peace, justice, order, good governance, the common good, accountable leadership, welfare, solidarity and subsidiarity, accountable leadership, – and the traits in our moral fabric that have constantly militated against them. Where the common good has been so blatantly orphaned, how do we expect to progress?

From these articles the reader is confronted with the plight of a country whose future is in freefall and needs redemption. Father George Ehusani has not tired of nudging the conscience of Nigerians to the possibility of the country to self-destruct. Like the visionary prophet, his warnings will only be ignored at our own peril as he constantly offers remedies and the way forward to peace, progress and prosperity.

The enduring season of lament notwithstanding, Father Ehusani reminds Nigerians not to yield to distress and despondency, and admonishes that hoping for better climes is a worthwhile engagement. Like a lone voice in the wilderness, this publication clamours for a change in focus and direction, a reversal from the suicidal slide toward the brink of collapse and disintegration, and a renewal of the soul of the nation. Ignoring the writer's dire warnings may well result in another publication – Yet some more years...

Greg Aiyemo
Editor-in-Chief of Lux Terra Publications
Lux Terra Leadership Foundation

Introduction

As a young professional twenty-five years ago, working in one of the most critical industries at the time, namely, the media, I witnessed an effervescent political climate that indicated hope. Then, amidst the growing infamy of a corrupt and draconian junta, students and workers, journalists and clerics, lawyers, and other professionals, formed a critical mass that courageously spoke truth to power. So combustive was the energy dissipated, so frontal was the consistent attack on the establishment, that the powerful voice of the people assumed the status of an alternative government. So united were the people in their sincerity of (a common) purpose, that watchers, who had some modicum of political insight, felt that in no time a bright light would appear at the end of the tunnel.

Today, every Nigerian adult, who has been a conscious witness to the state of affairs in the country in those twenty-five years, would have realised with utmost bitterness, if not helplessness, their incapacitation to salvage a country from distress. For many in this category, the story of Nigeria in the last three decades seems like a tragic tale of a country heading uncontrollably towards a self-directed path of destruction. Yet when one considers the array of luminaries with which the country is endowed, or the tenacity and resilience of Nigeria's teeming population, let alone Nigeria's so much talked about abundant resources, it becomes inconsolably painful how before one's very eyes we have begun to expire with the country.

How did the country degenerate to such a level of decadence? Is it the case that Nigerians did not work hard enough for the transformation of the country? Or has the country always been in this state of confusion? Is it not for the reason of the present state of crass ineptitude and cluelessness that our leaders are derided by those whom Henri Nouwen calls a 'Generation without fathers'? Is it a case of the absence of constructive social crusading? For the sake of millennial Nigerians of the Naira Marley generation, who covet the pervasive lawlessness and indiscipline as the new norm, or for the discerning ones among them who curse the old legion that threw them into this facticity of hopelessness, there is a need for frank talk to disabuse crooked perception. Such dialogue should let this Generation X know that the modicum of sanity being enjoyed today has come from the courage and tenacity of consistent dreamers of peace and love. It should let them know that they too could become hopeful dreamers whose collective action may someday beget a civilisation of love. Furthermore, such dialogue should remind older Nigerians whose sense of history has been fossilised by fear and amnesia that all hope is not lost, and cannot be lost; that a miracle still beckons from the audacity of hope.

Thus, in fidelity to the demands of truth and our national well-being, there is a need for actors and witnesses to our socio-historical evolution to present narratives of the times from their peculiar perspectives. Like all other agencies of mobilisation and social action, religious bodies or faith-based organisations have been active agents of social change through the routine activities of clerics and members, and in the good works carried out by groups in such organisations. For those in the Christian Church, certain events in society demand that there be a more forceful but sombre engagement with society so as to re-direct the course of social evolution towards its best possible destination. To do this requires prophets who would put their comfort and their very lives on the line to speak for the people and speak to power.

One of such prophetic voices is that of Rev. Fr. George Omaku Ehusani. During the critical moments of recent national history, especially those years characterised by the inglorious years of the Babangida-Abacha military dictatorships, Ehusani was a prominent actor in the drama of contemporary Nigerian struggle. He joined other members of the critical mass that brought the draconian and terrorising junta of those years to its knees. Those were the days when the petrels of constructive criticism rained from every corner of the country against the Neroic obstinacy of the ruling junta. Because the injustice and oppression of the junta knew no socio-political or ethno-religious barrier, it touched everyone who had a sense of justice.

We had among numerous others Bala Usman, M. D. Yusufu, Adamu Ciroma, Balarabe Musa and Col. Abubakar Dangiwa Umar from the north; we had Pini Jason, John Nwodo, Chidi Ubani, Clement Nwankwo and Olisa Agbakoba from the eastern part of the country. We had Pa Alfred Rewane, Ken Saro-Wiwa, Ledum Mitee and Frank Kokori from the Niger-Delta. From the southwest came a garrison of strange bedfellows, all unified by a common agenda to save the country from the perdition plotted by the junta. The list is long. Even clerics, a section of which was led by the then Catholic Archbishop of Lagos, Anthony Olubunmi Okogie, found a moral obligation to join this critical mass.

Among this amorphous crowd of critics was Fr. Ehusani, who, having been posted to the Catholic Secretariat of Nigeria in Lagos at the time, rekindled his passion for constructive social engagement. About five years before this time, Ehusani had tested the efficacy of public engagement with authority when he successfully carried out a one-man protest, against the then Kogi State government over non-payment of teachers' salaries. Thus, coming to Lagos, the national epicentre of civil society protests, indicated wider latitude for engagement. With Rev. Fr. Matthew Hassan Kukah (now Bishop Kukah), he formed a tag team from the Christian religious community that provided Christocentric and ecclesial relevance to the struggle for change. From that moment on, Ehusani seemed to have pieced together all his endowment – talent, time, treasure, intellect, emotion and energy – into a veritably powerful instrument of spiritual conversation.

The final cause of his engagement was, justifiably, spiritual conversion because, transcending the sectarian confines of religious or political conversion, it hit at the core of humanity – the consciousness, culture and values that are dispensed in bettering the lot of the human person. As he churned out articles, essays, poems, speeches and homilies, he did not make such missives products from casual exercises of a hobby. Rather, like consummate illuminates who have made writing a course of duty to transform human civilisation, he committed himself to the life-long task of educating, guiding, leading and sharing.

This volume, *Nigeria: More Years Eaten By The Locusts*, is a documentation of 31 selected presentations made by Fr. George in the course of his priestly life, especially the twenty-year period of 1998 to 2018. The collection comprises articles and papers lamenting the situation of our country during the many more years devoured by the locusts. It holds thought-provoking theological and philosophical reflections on existential challenges confronting Nigeria and its people. It contains articles, essays, homilies, speeches, seasonal spiritual reflections, addresses to secular authorities, briefings to the media, papers delivered at various forums – all of which examine or analyse wide-ranging issues that affect Nigeria's political and socio-economic space such as the search for a just social order, constructive engagement between religion and politics, morality and society, human rights, the imperative of socio-ethical behaviour transformation, and the leadership question.

A random selection of articles from *Nigeria: More Years Eaten By The Locusts* would reveal the resurgence of maladies that have afflicted Nigerians in the years before, some of which were reflected upon in an earlier collection of articles, published in the year 2002 under the title, *"Nigeria: Years Eaten By the Locusts."* Now let us look at Chapter One of this new publication, titled, "When God Is Not to Blame." Written in the context of the death of two illustrious Nigerian politicians, Chief Moshood Abiola and

Gen. Shehu Yar'Adua (rtd), both of whom died in prison custody, this essay decries the warped theological thinking that attributed the mishaps to divine will. Expressing his aversion to this dubious ascription, Ehusani states: "Both men died as victims of the primordial greed and satanic ogre of the fallen angels that constituted what someone has called the 'luciferian regime' of the late General Sani Abacha. Many of our present leaders were part and parcel of that demonic dispensation that decreed blood and tears for Nigerians." Although he criticises the military junta for this, he, in the next chapter titled "Nigeria: The Struggle Continues", cautions that the installation of President Olusegun Obasanjo in a renascent democratic regime does not guarantee an end to this profligacy and misuse of power. Ehusani would be proven right as the next article making up Chapter 3, "Salisu Buhari as a Metaphor," seems to illustrate the metaphor of lies and deceit that Nigeria had become with the new dispensation.

As if to ward off the ominous trailing of this new political dispensation, especially as the new millennium approached, Ehusani penned "A Jubilee Year Prayer for Peace" contained in Chapter 4. Like his customary prayerful reflections, which he dishes out in festive seasons, the Jubilee Year prayer heralding the new millennium provided opportunities for sober moments of recollections amidst the giddiness of mundane pursuits. He goes on in Chapter 5 to expose the moral problem of neglecting the common good, and in the next chapter calls for the transformation of Nigeria's traumatising prisons to correctional centres. Against the backdrop of the fatal fire incident that engulfed poor oil scoopers in rural Jesse, Delta State, Ehusani in Chapter 7 declares the Niger Delta as Nigeria's guilt and shame. He also expresses this same sentiment in Chapter 8, where he uses the famed Oputa Panel to raise questions about our sanity. Further on, in Chapter 9 he sustains his incredulity towards our social values in "The Abuse of National Honours and Chieftaincy Titles."

Given the divisive instrumentalisation of religion that characterises the Nigerian society today, many readers may relate well with Chapters 10 and 11 respectively, titled "The Sharia and Religious Persecution in Nigeria" and "A Review of the Sharia Crisis in Nigeria". In these essays Ehusani examines the historical roots of religious persecution in Nigeria, the main issues surrounding the manifestation of persecution, and the challenges a country like Nigeria faces in the light of its constitutional status as a secular state. All this is set within the context of the introduction of the Sharia Law and its subsequent adoption by many states in Northern Nigeria at the time. Ehusani later ascribes this phenomenon to fanaticism, which he dubs a challenge to Nigeria. The irrationality of fananticism, as the article in Chapter 14 explicates, is hinged on the fact that a psychotic adherent expends incredible efforts on a religion whose doctrines and practices he hardly understands. Other articles include: "The Status of Education", "Help! Maniacs in Power", "The Problem with Nigeria", "Beyond the Politics of Acrimony and Absurdity."

Another article deserving of careful reading is Chapter 17, "The Nigeria Police and Our Moral Degeneracy." Considering the widespread insecurity characterised by escalating threat to safety, routine impunity, the failure of the law and the triumph of injustice, this article examines the parody of law enforcement which the Nigerian Police have become. In a detailed analysis of the painful encounters between the police and the citizen, as well as the negative image rendered by this analysis, Ehusani finds no justification for their abuse of power. He submits: "The conduct of our Police Officers in Nigeria has not only legal but also moral implications for us. To whatever extent the allegations against officers of the Nigeria Police are correct, there are ethical or moral issues that are involved in the intimidation and extortion of innocent Nigerians."

In the next six essays, Ehusani discusses, once again, the manipulation of religion for political ends and the resultant moral vacuity it creates both for the individual and the polity. In the light of the moral vacuum caused by corruption, greed, ethnic cum religious intolerance, and indiscipline, Ehusani castigates what he calls the troubling environment of contemporary Nigerian religiosity and its agents for their charlatanism and de-spiritualisation of the Christian faith. In the same vein, he condemns the incessant exploitation of youths as cannon fodder for religious crises, political mayhem and unreasonable protests. His bitter reflection on this exploitative tendency is captured in the article, "Youth Restiveness, Social Instability, and the Quest for Peace in a Democratic Nigeria". This is followed by others treating state failure, leadership, the culture of impunity and an open letter to President Olusegun Obasanjo titled "Dancing On the Brink of Disaster".

In the last part of this collection, he concentrates on the question of leadership as the social need at the time, namely an election season requiring new sets of political leaders, demanded such a reaction. Thus, it is understandable that the essays would feature such titles as 'The Challenge of Leadership', 'Of Rogues, Gangsters and Politicians', 'Flawed Elections and the Challenge of Nation Building', 'Nigeria: Missing Ingredients of

Nation Building', 'Elite Conspiracy in the Nigerian National Ruination', and 'National Unity and the Application of the Federal Character Principle'.

Finally, the dubious appeal to the supernatural that defines the paradox of our value system is further re-echoed in Chapter 30 titled, "Booming Religiosity and Rampant Corruption in Nigeria: Our Moral Conundrum". In this article Ehusani explores the blatant contradiction telegraphed by our rapacious taste for shallow religiosity while still wallowing in the cesspool of corruption. To fend off this apparent contradiction, Ehusani highlights the inimitable values of religion to the individual and the society. That Nigerians make so much noise about religion does not mean that corruption and religion are bedfellows. In Chapter 31 "Role of Religion in Curbing Corruption," he not only shows how antithetical corruption is to religion, but also spells out out strategies by which religion should help in the fight against corruption. Foremost of these strategies is his call for a rescue mission rooted in a revitalised evangelisation and moral education. And for Christians it is the call to be the light of the world.

Some Comments

From the above analysis it could be observed that the arrangement of this collection of articles follows a deliberate chronological order for some reasons. Firstly, this historical order allows readers to follow the trails of events of the time in question, that is, 1998 to 2018. In other words, as one reads the work from one chapter to another, one would be able to relate the discussion or issues raised by the author to real life events in history. In this regard, the issues raised in this collection presuppose that the monstrosities of yesteryears have trailed us, or rather have mutated exponentially, as they followed us all these years.

The mendacity and perfidy that characterised the years of the locust are brazenly exhibited in today's Nigeria. Broken promises, outright lies, deliberate falsehoods have become the norms guiding the administrative ethos of today's ruling elite. The wanton pillaging and thievery that made Nigerians shudder in shock during the Babangida-Abacha years have become the casual lifestyle of today's ruling elite. It is now an honour to be a squanderer of government funds and to celebrate obscene wealth with pomp and religious ritual. Rather than being vilified for criminal appropriation and immodest extravagance, a political thief and plunderer gets social recognition sometimes with church knighthood and traditional chieftaincy titles.

No time has Nigeria been so religiously polarised in the most acrimonious and barbaric manner as today. From the quantum of articles on religion, it could be inferred that the seed of discord that has sprouted into widespread insecurity today was watered by the blood and sweat of victims of religious fanaticism. No time has Nigeria been so epistemically delusional in terms of religious values and morals as in today's Nigeria. There seems to be a determined effort to carry out a destructive transvaluation of the noble qualities that built this great country. It is for this reason that this collection rightly deserves the title it has been given, *Nigeria: More Years Eaten by the Locust.*

What is Fr. George Ehusani saying by bringing this book to the public space? Firstly, he is demonstrating that he is a prophetic witness to our chequered historicity. A patient reading of this collection shows that Fr. George Ehusani has witnessed the moral despoliation and pillaging of the last thirty years, twenty of which he has written about. Just as he was challenged by the Nigeria of yesteryears, so also are we compelled by the demands of posterity to act and be witnesses to the present struggle. Today, more than ever before, there is an uncanny alliance amongst the various categories of oppressors against the weak and vulnerable. More than ever before, we are witnessing a bolder replay of the same perversion of over two decades ago. Grand corruption is displayed as statecraft, primitive accumulation and scandalous gratification are rationalised as legal entitlements in a country in dire economic straits.

Besides, the country is witnessing its worst security challenges. We are engulfed by wars from all fronts: the murderous and irrational Boko Haram insurgents, the senseless killings by Fulani Herdsmen, killer-bandits and kidnappers. All this happens at a time law enforcement and security agencies claim to be at their best. Thus, it seems, nothing happening today should shock Nigerians. Everything happening now has been foreshadowed by the deliberate misdeeds and inexcusable actions of yesterday's leaders and followers.

Secondly, the narratives in the collection portray Nigerians as incurably foolhardy and *alliterate* to warning signs; signs that have emanated from wise prognosis of our social condition. A dangerous fideism is pervading our social space imbuing into us the strange confidence that in spite of prophetic warning signs all will be well. As the witty American philosopher George Santayana wrote about the trite repeatability of history: "Those who cannot remember the past are condemned to repeat it." And this repetition has consequences. One thing which Ehusani's collection inspires is the hard lesson inherent in Santayana's catchy aphorism above. When a people refuse to learn from history, they pursue their own self destruction in a very determined way. Nigeria has inflicted on its people gratuitous harm from their indolence and imperviousness to heed the lessons of history. We may fail to heed this one too, and head towards further harm.

Notwithstanding this not-so-cheering introduction, *Nigeria: More Years Eaten By The Locusts* should not be viewed as a spiteful representation of the country; one that condemns Nigeria to eternal perdition and an irredeemable end. Rather it should be considered as a narrative that should jolt Nigerians to seek how to teach younger generations honest history about this country. It should teach the truth that one who does not know their past cannot plot the trajectory of their future.

It should open us to the realization that if we, as a country and as fellows, are to be expurgated from the ongoing locust invasion, there is need for some moral fumigation, by injecting the system with men and women who have in a determined way decided to sacrifice themselves for thorough cleansing. A takeaway message here is this: It takes extensive moral leadership and determined construction of moral filters to rake out of the system the debris of the years of pestilence.

Anthony Okeregbe
Department of Philosophy, University of Lagos, Nigeria

CHAPTER ONE

When God Is Not to Blame
(Written on July 25, 1998)

The dust seems to have settled and it is business as usual once again for my countrymen and women renowned for their incredibly short attention span. Perhaps it is a virtue that Nigerians, anxious as they are to move the nation forward, often quickly put things behind them. Yet I have strong reasons to suspect that they are only postponing the doomsday, because their determination to move the nation forward is not an indication that past hurts are forgiven, or that the wounds inflicted by the injustices of the past are sufficiently healed. That is why the Nigerian landscape is presently constituted by multiple layers of resentment, which, if not adequately addressed through such fora as "Failed Governments Tribunal," "Truth and Reconciliation Committee," or "Sovereign National Conference," may degenerate in future into a crisis of monumental proportion such as the world has witnessed recently in Rwanda and in Bosnia.

The death of Chief M. K. O. Abiola on Tuesday July 7, 1998, after four long years of humiliation at the hands of the military remains for me a source of grave concern. Coming barely seven months after the passing away of General Shehu Yar'adua in the Abakaliki prison where he had been kept by those who must rule Nigeria by force of arms, the death of Abiola should rightly provoke nationwide outrage against the military which has brutally wasted the lives of some of our best countrymen and women, and recklessly plundered, looted and vandalised our entire nation state. Nigerians have been told that Abiola died of natural causes. That is to say that those who did the autopsy could demonstrate that he was not shot, that he was not blown apart by a bomb, or that he was not poisoned.

The report of the experts indicate that he died of "severe long-standing diseases of the heart." But does this absolve the military of blame? Should they not accept responsibility for his death? Does the report of the autopsy not confirm the allegation that civilians are usually subjected to unjust and inhuman treatment in military detention centres? Is Chief Abiola's death not just one more in what has become a daily occurrence in our overcrowded and decrepit prisons and detention centres where human beings, our kith and kin, are meant to die by instalment? A Human Rights Organisation published a report two years ago indicating that at least one prisoner died every week at the *Kirikiri* Maximum Security prison in Lagos, due to acute neglect, abuse or torture.

Recently the Head of State paid a condolence visit to the Abiola family, and like Muhammed Marwa the Administrator of Lagos State and other spokesmen of the military who have gone before him, General Abubakar blamed the death of Abiola on "God's will." He said it was an act of God which must be accepted as such, since no one could question God. He said it was unfortunate that this incident occurred when Abiola was about to be released. I noticed that there was no word of apology from him on behalf of the military. There was no indication that he considered the military responsible for the death of the presumed winner of the 1993 presidential election.

The impression given by the Head of State and others in his immediate constituency is that no one could be blamed for the death of Chief Abiola, since it was purely an act of God. But are Nigerians today convinced that Chief Moshood Abiola did not die of acute neglect at the hands of his captors? For the four years he was kept unjustly behind bars, have Nigerians been sufficiently convinced that he ate the kind of food which his delicate health condition required? Have the authorities demonstrated to us that during the period of his incarceration he was provided with adequate space and such amenities for physical exercise which his impaired heart required? Have we been told that in those four years when he was in government custody, he had free access to the standard of medical care he could afford?

Chief Abiola was said to have passed some of his prison notes to a member of his family. In those notes which were published in their original form in some of the National Dailies, Chief Abiola complained of acute under-nourishment and poor medical attention. His own testimony indicated that he was detained in a poorly ventilated and poorly lighted room, with no space for physical exercise. Thus, if indeed Abiola suffered an expansion of the heart while in prison, then can it not be said that the appalling conditions of the prison, coupled with the emotional and psychological cost of the humiliation at the hands of the military accelerated his death?

Nigerians are very religious people. They believe in the supremacy of God's will. They are very quick to attribute tragic occurrences to the will of

God. But that disposition is being exploited today by those who have always played games with the fortunes of our people. The Nigerian people have been told once again to accept the sudden death of Abiola after four years in detention as God's will. But the death of Moshood Abiola in government custody, like that of General Shehu Yar'Adua, is one of those events that cannot be attributed to the will of God without some qualification, unless religion is once again to be used as the opium of the people. The good Lord is not the author of evil, and so cannot take responsibility for tragedies that are a direct consequence of the moral choices of free human agents.

The Lord God certainly foresees all that will happen long before they take place - the good, the bad, and the ugly. He sometimes permits evil, because of the freedom which he bestowed on the human person at creation, but he does not "will" evil. It is not in the nature of the good God to will evil. What is referred to as an "act of God" in classical Christian thought is an event that cannot be blamed on the wickedness, carelessness or neglect of a human agent. Natural disasters, certain category of accidents, and such diseases and sicknesses that occur irrespective of the society's commitment to provide a healthy environment or the individual's efforts to lead a healthy lifestyle, belong to this group. Other tragedies are often a consequence of the free act of a moral agent. They are therefore a moral evil, and moral evils cannot be attributed to God.

If Yar'Adua and Abiola passed away the time they did due to acute neglect or abuse during the long period of their incarceration under sub-human conditions, then their death could not be said to be the will of God, but the direct consequence of the mischievous acts of fellow human beings. God does not will that innocent people should be locked up for years under sub-human conditions and subjected to all forms of torture. God does not will that one person should assume the power of life and death over another, trading in fake coups and dangling the sword of treason before all potential political opponents. God does not will that one person should humiliate another even up to the point of death. The fact that the wicked succeeded in their evil machination certainly means that God foresaw it, since he is omniscient. He must have permitted it, otherwise it would not happen. But does this amount to saying that God "willed" it? No, my own God does not "will" evil.

The Head of State and his collaborators, and indeed all Nigerians should take note that the circumstances surrounding the death of General Shehu Yar'Adua and Chief Moshood Abiola are such that the good Lord cannot be held responsible. Both men died as victims of the primordial greed and satanic ogre of the fallen angels that constituted what someone has called the "luciferian regime" of the late General Sani Abacha. Many of our present leaders were part and parcel of that demonic dispensation that decreed blood and tears for Nigerians. That is why I believe the military should take responsibility for the death of the two influential politicians and the numerous others who are not so well known and tender an unreserved apology to Nigerians for their war crimes against fellow citizens even at peace time.

Nigerians are familiar with quacks and charlatans who operate as priests, pastors, prophets and evangelists. Yet on serious matters, they know who to believe. The antecedents of the military are such that they are today the least qualified to preach to us about God and His divine will. Instead of further provoking right-thinking Nigerians and insulting our collective intelligence with preachments and pious exhortations on the "will of God" or "the act of God," what we truly deserve from the military is an unreserved apology that will elicit such forgiveness and reconciliation as will put the nation on the path of lasting peace and prosperity.

CHAPTER TWO

Nigeria: The Struggle Continues
(Written on June 7, 1999)

A change has at last occurred in our political landscape after a sixteen-year nightmarish transition that seemed eternal damnation. Though the dramatis personae do not inspire too much confidence as they are largely recycled from the old corrupt and discredited brigade, nevertheless many of our countrymen and women see the successful conclusion of the elections and the swearing-in ceremonies of our Local Government Councillors and Chairmen, our State Legislators and Governors, and members of the House of Representatives, Senators and the President, as one big step forward in our journey towards a free, democratic, united, peaceful and prosperous society. For this achievement we congratulate ourselves and praise the good Lord who makes things happen. The event of May 29, 1999 was indeed the Lord's doing, and it is marvelous in our eyes.

The installation of Olusegun Obasanjo as civilian president on May 29, 1999, was preceded by extravagant luncheons and parties, at which occasions our expert sycophants and executive clowns were on hand to inflate the egos of the retiring commanders of the Nigerian army and nation, for surrendering power to their civilian allies after nearly sixteen years of rogue leadership, the extent of whose looting and pillage of the land is legendary. There are aspects of the "send-off" parades, luncheons and parties which for me bordered on mediocrity on the part of the ordinary citizens and vanity on the part of the retiring generals. Nigerians who on those occasions canonized Abdulsalami Abubakar and his team for handing over power to an elected president seem to forget that the military could hold on to power in Nigeria only for as long as Nigerians wanted them to. If we have truly arrived at democratic governance in Nigeria, it is not out of the goodwill of a band of generals, but rather that the time's up for the military.

Now for General Abubakar and his group, the bazaar may be over, but not for Obasanjo and the generality of Nigerians for whom the struggle must continue. We may have won the battle, but we have certainly not won the war. The installation is only the beginning of what may turn out to be a long-drawn battle to rid Nigeria of the remnants of primitive feudalism, ethnic warlords, callous mercenaries, greedy scavengers, military adventurists and those shameless sycophants, mindless opportunists and reckless prostitutes of power, who, over the years, have conspired to render Nigeria desolate and its people destitute.

Indeed, many of those elected and appointed into political positions today along with their sponsors cannot be trusted to lead us to the promised land, if their antecedents are anything to go by. That they got to the present positions is in many cases not a tribute to their personal integrity, wholesome nationalism or high sense of patriotism. We know too well that across the length and breadth of this country, elective positions often went to the highest bidder, even if the individual be an established rogue.

Yet, with the successful installation of a civilian president, long-suffering Nigerians who have experience many painful bouts of broken promises and dashed hopes, once again have their hopes rekindled. Abused and deceived for the umpteenth time in the recent past, resilient Nigerians are once again looking forward to a change in their fortunes. They are hoping that with the swearing in of a participatory government on May 29, the dream of freedom and well-being which they nurtured before 1979, before 1993, and since June 1998, will finally be realised. They are hoping that the military, which had become an occupation force, would finally return to the barracks and remain there forever, unless they are called out to defend the territorial boundaries of the nation. They are hoping that the physical withdrawal of the military to the barracks, will mark the end of the command culture and the superstructure of violence that has sent countless Nigerians to their early graves, and condemned the others to an existence of misery.

Survivors of the Nigerian military profligacy are hoping that the return of the soldiers to the barracks will bring an end to the kleptocracy that has characterised Nigerian governance in the last few decades, culminating in the rogue dispensation of the late General Sani Abacha. They are hoping that there will be stability in the polity, and that with this, foreign investors will be attracted to Nigeria, and thus the comatose economy will bounce back to life. Nigerians are hoping that General Obasanjo and his comrades will play out their roles as honourable statesmen and women, and deliver on their promise of fairness, probity and accountability in governance. Nigerians are right to keep hoping in this way, for otherwise they would self-destruct. Yet relying wholly on the goodwill of the recently elected politicians for the emergence of an accountable, democratic government and the evolution of a just, peaceful and prosperous nation would be foolhardy. It would be the height of naivety for Nigerians to build their tall hopes on the band of politicians who have found their way into the various legislative and executive positions in the nation's government machinery, for by and large, they are the same characters whose greed for money and lust for power, and whose blindness and insensitivity to the common good, has brought the giant of Africa to its knees, making the erstwhile proud Nigerians to lick the dust.

Thus, after God, the responsibility of turning the nation around cannot be placed on the shoulders of these same characters, even when they have used their loot to buy up exalted positions in the new dispensation. They possess neither the moral authority nor the political will to truly turn things around. And a fundamental change in the socio-economic and political landscape will not be in their interest. The responsibility of turning things around will rest at the doorpost of the various components of civil society. It is the civil society that should immediately get to work and set the agenda for the new civilian administration, recognising that they are not at the mercy of the professional politicians who once again have wangled their way into top positions. True, the generality of Nigerians must quickly wake up to the fact that they are not at the mercy of professional politicians, whether of the military or civilian variant. In the modern society, it is understood that sovereignty belongs to the generality of the people, not to a few ethnic warlords, oil sheiks, treasury looters or military conquerors.

The Labour Unions, the Bar Association, the Judiciary, the Students, Professional Groups, the Churches, the numerous Human Rights Advocacy Groups that now abound, should constitute themselves into watchmen for democracy and justice, watchmen for accountability and transparency, and watchmen for the responsible management of the economy and conduct of politics. The organs of civil society are the ones to sit up and hold the feet of the politicians as close as possible to the fire of democracy. For the realisation of our dream of a just, peaceful and prosperous nation, the generality of Nigerians shall have to abandon their accustomed apathy and despondency. Unless we transform ourselves from an apathetic to a pro-active citizenry, the mere change of uniform or change of baton will not take us to the promised land. Yes, we must assert our rights as free people, and insist on our prerogative to set the agenda for the new government, if our new-found hope is not to be dashed once again.

Above all, if we are to arrive at the promised land, Nigerians and their leaders must come to recognise that greed and avarice are a cancer that eats its own host to death; that corruption ultimately kills not only the victims, but also the perpetrators; and that unless we change our course we are bound to end up where we are headed. To arrive at the destination of our dream, Nigerians and their leaders must come to recognise that lies, manipulation, and political subterfuge have never, and will never nurture a people; that thievery, robbery and roguery, by whatever name else it is called, when it becomes king in a land, that land rots; and when hooliganism and banditry get into high places, the superstructure soon comes crashing down. To facilitate the emergence of a peaceful and prosperous nation, Nigerians and their leaders must recognise that where lawlessness becomes the norm, and illegality becomes the rule, the nation collapses; that righteousness exalts a nation, but that sin is a reproach to a people; and that where there is no vision the people soon perish. When we as a people decide to wake up to these realities and live by these truths, our land shall by the grace of the good Lord experience a rejuvenation, and the giant of Africa shall once again bounce back on its feet.

CHAPTER THREE

Salisu Buhari as a Metaphor
(Written on July 23, 1999)

Former Speaker of the House of Representatives, Alhaji Salisu Buhari has turned out to be the first major casualty of the new democratic dispensation in Nigeria. Barely seven weeks into the new administration, Alhaji Buhari has had to resign from the position of Speaker and member of the House of Representatives, following the shocking discovery by The News Magazine that Alhaji Buhari had falsified his age and lied about his educational qualification.

Relying on records relating to his admission into and graduation from King's College, Lagos, the Magazine was able to establish that Alhaji Buhari should be 29 years and not 36 years of age. The implication is that he did not qualify to seek elective position in the nation's House of Assembly. Also, after series of phone and fax exchanges between the Magazine and the University of Toronto which Alhaji Buhari claims to have attended, the Magazine was able to establish that the Speaker has no university degree in Business Administration as he claims in his curriculum vitae. Thus, he was exposed to Nigerians as a fraud who does not merit the exalted position of the Speaker of the House of Representatives.

The exposure of Alhaji Buhari might be seen as a major victory for the new democratic dispensation where probity, accountability and press freedom are cardinal virtues. While Nigeria was under the dictatorship of the gun, such humiliation of a senior public official would have been inconceivable, for the Magazine would never have seen the light of day, and the authors of the "subversive publication" would most surely have ended up in one of the nation's torture chambers. True, for nearly sixteen years Nigeria succumbed to the monumental fraud of a Babangida and an Abacha who transformed roguery, banditry, and gangsterism into a high art, made falsehood a state policy and lying an instrument of governance, and polluted the various organs of society with the poisonous venom of corruption. The public humiliation of Alhaji Buhari therefore might be seen as a major victory for President Olusegun Obasanjo's anti-corruption crusade, even as the nation's parliament is still debating the proposed anti-corruption bill.

The News Magazine which brought the Buhari fraud to light has earned a unique recognition for championing in this new dispensation what we might call "prosecutorial journalism." Those journalists and other gentlemen of the press who joined in the public prosecution of the Speaker deserve to be congratulated. The critical elements among our law makers who (amidst strong opposition from their colleagues) moved and supported the motion for an investigation into the fraud, and the generality of Nigerians that insisted on knowing the truth, also deserve to be congratulated. Yet for me the celebrated fraud of the Speaker of the House of Representatives speaks volumes for the degree of social dis-equilibrium in our country. The shameful story of Buhari is only an index of the social pathology of the Nigerian who seeks wealth, power and position by any means, foul or fair. Yes, the Buhari saga, however embarrassing, is a true manifestation of the extent of moral degeneration and social decay among the Nigerian elite, and the utter lack of scruples among Nigerian politicians.

For me, Buhari is a metaphor for the bundle of lies or the monumental deceit which the Nigerian nation has become. Buhari accentuates the Nigerian propensity to deceive, to defraud and to falsify. Many of those who went to town over Buhari, demanding his impeachment, asking for his prosecution, and calling for his conviction and imprisonment, are themselves ironically thriving in palaces of fraud, sitting on thrones of deceit and wearing crowns made out of lies.

Nigerians in high and low places have elevated lying to a royal art whose suzerainty is manifested in fraud, forgery, deceit, falsification, perjury, prevarication, equivocation, distortion, counterfeiting, simulation and frame-ups. We lie as individuals as well as corporate bodies. Our governments are often the worst liars. We lie by falsifying our age, obtaining dubious birth and death certificates, swearing to false affidavits and taking solemn oaths in courts with the Bible or Quran in our hands, knowing fully well that we do not mean what we are saying.

We lie by falsifying census figures, manipulating votes and rigging elections. We lie by the way we engage in various shades of examination malpractice, forging certificates and awarding ourselves dubious academic titles. We lie by parading ourselves as professors, doctors and lawyers even when we have never been within the walls of a university. We lie by forging signatures, inflating contract figures, and falsifying invoices and cash receipts. We lie by giving clearance papers for jobs that have not been properly executed. We lie by issuing dud cheques - even government departments and corporate organisations are often guilty of this criminal practice.

We lie by falsifying the weights and measures with which we sell gari and rice or beans. We lie by selling fake drugs and fake spare parts. We lie by obtaining fresh drivers' licenses without the requisite driving tests. We lie by obtaining fake medical reports of fitness and obtaining sick leave certificates from doctors, when we are not qualified for such. We lie by obtaining fake entry visas to foreign countries that we must visit or migrate to at all costs. We lie by obtaining marriage certificates when we were never married. We even lie by bleaching our skin pigmentation in order to appear fairer than nature made us.

Our public wage system in this country is itself a fraudulent enterprise. What do we make of a salary structure where the highest placed civil servants in our ministries have a total take-home pay of less than two hundred thousand naira per annum, yet we know that many senior civil servants live in houses that cost more than ten million naira, they are allocated cars that cost more than three million naira, they use choice hotels that cost more than ten thousand naira for one night, and they make enough money from government to build mansions and send their children to schools and colleges in the United States and Britain, with bills running into millions of naira. The same government is able to tell poor Nigerian workers that it cannot pay three thousand naira to the least of its workers. Is this not a grand deception?

If there should be any sincere attempt at probing the credentials and conduct of public figures in Nigeria, the result will be a staggering discovery, since corruption in all its ramifications had long assumed the character and status of a national system which some people cynically refer to as "the Nigerian factor." Fraudsters are thriving because the environment is fraud-friendly. That is why I maintain that Buhari is a metaphor for the Nigerian state of moral decay. As we celebrate this scandal in our practised hypocrisy and pharisaism, we must for a moment reflect on our own soiled hands and lips, and as individuals and groups work towards conversion to a lifestyle of truth, which alone will bring lasting peace, unity and prosperity.

CHAPTER FOUR

A Jubilee Year Prayer
(Written on January 1, 2000)

As the year 2000 dawns, we raise our hands and voices in praise and thanksgiving, and we bow and bend our knee before you Almighty God, King of eternity, Lord of history and Designer of time. As we wake up to a new day, a new year, a new century, and ah, a new millennium, we praise and thank you for the wonder of your being, the miracle of our lives and the mystery of your love. We bow and bend our knee before you Father of Love, who, despite the extent of human depravity have not despaired of the world nor given up on men and women. We adore and bless your name, for the good news of the incarnation, celebrated in hope by the prophets of old and manifested at the most blessed of all times in Bethlehem. As we mark 2000th anniversary of this central event of history, we declare a celebration, we announce a year-long sabbath, yes, we proclaim a jubilee year, during which we are committed to the reconciliation of humanity and the restoration of creation.

Lord of all history, the twentieth century was one fraught with multiple paradoxes or mixed blessings. On the one hand the century witnessed such scientific and technological development as was never dreamt of before now. Sophisticated health care facilities, space travel, satellite communication, the computer, and the Internet, are some of the indexes of the technological breakthrough of that century. On the other hand, Lord, the twentieth century witnessed two of the most gruesome wars of human history – the first and the second world wars. The century witnessed genocide of unprecedented dimension in Rwanda, in Bosnia, in Liberia, in Sierra-Leone, and in the former territory of Yugoslavia.

For the African continent, the twentieth century was one in which things fell apart and the centre could not hold. Traditional values, including those related to the inviolability of life, the integrity of marriage and the sanctity of the family, all collapsed before the turbulent wind of modernity. Our own country recorded in the twentieth century a bitter civil war in which over one million lives were lost. And in the dying days of that century when many Nigerians believed that they were living through peace times, thousands of lives were lost in violent ethnic skirmishes, and through banditry, robbery and hired assassinations. You see Lord that the twentieth century ended with tension and strife in many lands and widespread fear and anxiety in the hearts of men and women, many of whom, in spite of widespread pretensions to religiosity, have continued to pursue a life of hatred, wickedness, idolatry, violence, greed, falsehood and injustice.

Lord we begin the Year 2000 on a note of realism. Our lofty expectations and grandiose projections in the last twenty-five years for a more wholesome humanity by the turn of the century have nearly all proved a mirage. Thus, "food for all by the year 2000," "housing for all by the year 2000," "adequate health care for all by the year 2000," and "literacy for all by the 2000," have become unrealisable, and we are back to the drawing board. As you know too well Lord, the year 1999 was for many of my countrymen and women another year of empty dreams, of broken promises and of dashed hopes. It brought for many a mixed bag of pain, grief, anxiety, fear, frustration, humiliation, resignation, despair, and a sprinkling of anticlimactic relief and ecstasy, brought about especially by your dramatic intervention in our national affairs on June 8, 1998, and ratified with the sweeping changes that took place in our political landscape on May 29, 1999 - changes however whose gains are yet to be felt by the common men and women across the land. That is why during the year, many of your faithful people intensified their "Prayer for Nigeria in Distress." Many even added for emphasis the new "Prayer Against Bribery and Corruption in Nigeria." They were waging a spiritual war as it were against the death-wish that reigned in the land in the form of bribery, corruption, and primordial greed.

You know Oh God of power and majesty that you have not finished your cleansing work among us, for all is not well with us yet. You are the God of peace, and your Son Jesus Christ is identified as the Prince of Peace. But what kind of peace can thrive in an environment of widespread poverty and destitution that have today assumed the moral equivalence of war? What kind of peace can we claim to have at a time when every essential commodity is scarce and priced beyond the reach of the average citizen? What kind of peace can we talk about in an era of gargantuan greed and conspicuous consumption that thrive side by side with acute deprivation? What manner of stability can we sustain in a land awash with ethnic bigotry and political buffoonery, where the constituent nationalities are ever at each other's throat and violence is erupting intermittently? What measure of security can we lay claim to in a society where the winner takes all, and where most of the people are often reduced to marginal existence?

What measure of security can we justifiably claim in this country with our ever increasing army of unemployed youths who have lost hope and meaning and who in desperation or despair are feeding on hard drugs, enlisting in satanic cults, and taking to street thuggery and armed robbery?

Omnipotent God and Lion of Judah, you are not known for half measures. You are not known to abandon your drowning faithful who cry to you mid-stream. Rather, faithfulness is in the very nature of your being. The Psalmist assures us that those who know you, who cling to your name, when they call upon you in time of distress you will be at their side to save them. We read in the book of Exodus that with a mighty hand you saw the oppressed children of Israel through the Red Sea dry shod while the chariots of their merciless pursuers perished in the swamp. When on Mount Carmel the corrupt devotees of Baal and Ashterot took on your servant Elijah, you did not abandon him in the hour of need. Instead, your vindication brought down a consuming fire. When at the sea of Galilee, the boat in which the disciples of Jesus were travelling was threatened by a violent storm, they were not abandoned to their fate. Your eternal Son spoke the word of power, and all was calm again. And when at a time of acute persecution your servants, Peter and John, cried to you from their prison cells, you did not look the other way. You miraculously loosened their bonds and threw open the gates of their jailhouse.

Visit our land Oh Lord during this Jubilee Year, this year of your favour, and convict the Nigerian elite of the life of debauchery by which they often elevated thievery into a high statecraft. Visit us this year and uproot the monumental pillars of greed and avarice, which constituted a pandemic national perversion that brought the nation to its knees in the wearied years of the last century. Visit us this year and weed clean from our national landscape the thorns and after-growths of systemic corruption that like noxious plants filled the entire environment with a poisonous stench. Visit us this year and dislodge completely the demon of kleptomania which in those years eaten by the locust, bestrode our land like a colossus, and led us along the dark alleys of economic depression, political anarchy, social disintegration, and international alienation.

Visit us this year, Jehovah God, and deliver us from blind guides, callous mercenaries and greedy opportunists who plunder the commonwealth with utter recklessness. Come and save our nation Nigeria from the hands of primitive feudalists, influence peddlers and contract chasers along with their agents and allies at all levels, who in the dying days of the twentieth century, camouflage as politicians. Breathe your almighty breath on us this Jubilee Year and flush out from our midst the pathological thieves, rogues and brigands whose persistent impulse to steal and to grab in the recent past rode in tandem with their inordinate ambition for power.

Come down Lord with your outstretched arm and destroy the myth of money and power, security, and invincibility, so that the corrupt elements that still litter our national landscape may give way permanently in order that uprightness may rise and flower in this country, and that the civilisation of love may blossom in these climes. Show the men and women of reason in Nigeria how to resist the temptation to apathy and despondency. Show us how to rise up and be counted on the side of reason, truth and justice. Show us how to refrain from joining the bandwagon in a life of greed and graft. Show us how to reject the foolish pattern of life which has led our nation to the mess of the recent past. Show us how to cultivate the virtues of love, truth, equity, justice, mutual forgiveness, discipline and patriotism, which alone can bring peace and prosperity. Show us that if today we begin to cultivate these virtues, then we would have laid the foundation for a more wholesome life in the new millennium.

Tear the heavens open and come down to us Oh God of Solomon. Draw the attention of our politicians to the fact so amply demonstrated in our recent history, that democracy is not synonymous with elections, and that elections do not necessarily bring peace. Teach us that democracy in its highest expression is the mutual acknowledgement of certain fundamental truths, including the truth of the dignity, equality, and freedom of all in a society. Impress upon Nigerians the lesson that democracy will only germinate and thrive upon the mutual recognition and acceptance of the truth that all the inhabitants of the geographical expression we call Nigeria, all who qualify to be called Nigerians by birth or naturalisation, must enjoy equal rights, dignity, and opportunities, irrespective of ethnic origin, religious affiliation, and political preference. Teach us the lesson that peace is only achieved by people who know and live by the fact that righteousness exalts a nation, but that greed, exploitation and oppression destroy a people. Help us to understand with Pope John Paul II that respect for human rights is the secret of lasting peace.

Make this Jubilee Year truly a year of favour, Oh God Almighty, and do ensure I pray the rejuvenation of the multitude whose life has been a calligraphy of agony and a mosaic of misery. Since in your tremendous love you have not despaired of Nigerians, and you wish to continue to do business with us, let the advent of a new year, a new century, and a new millennium signal the birth of a new hope that will illumine the portal of death and dispel the cloud of despair that hovered over those who hungered for truth and thirsted for justice in the dying days of the last century. Eternal Father and Ancient of Days, at the dawn of creation you breathed your Spirit upon the formless void and brought order out of the primordial chaos. Let the dawn of the Jubilee Year bring a sudden twist in fate for those in our country who on the eve of this century gracefully sowed their tears and invested their sorrows in your loving hands. Wipe away the tears of the many who weep on daily basis in our country.

God of mercy and compassion, let there be a change in fortune this Jubilee Year for long-standing victims of injustice. Bring about a veritable change in the lot of those who have suffered persecution or discrimination, those who are lonely, and those who are abandoned or rejected. Yes Lord, the prophets know you as the Friend of the Poor, Father of the Orphan and Defender of the Widow. In the Magnificat the Virgin Mary identified you as the one who pulls down the mighty and raises up the lowly. You are the same yesterday, today and forever, so let those who are pushed to the margins of our society by the strong and powerful find comfort and consolation in your jubilee visitation and restoration. Let those who in their tribulation have held on to your Word and faithfully awaited your powerful intervention not be disappointed in this Jubilee Year. Forbid it Lord that the flood of tears of those who toiled and grieved in hope should end up in the ocean of decay. No Lord, not this year of favour. Make it possible in the Jubilee Year that those who sowed in tears will reap in joy. Make it possible that their pool of tears will become a valuable resource to be transformed into an oasis of fortune.

Visit us in the year 2000 Lord, and lead us through the process of restoration, for that is what the biblical Jubilee is all about. Make all things new in our own day as you promised in the Book of Revelation. Fulfil the promise you made through the Prophet Ezekiel that "I will give them one heart and put a new spirit within them; I will take the stony heart out of their bodies and give them a heart of flesh..." In this year of favour, Oh God of Majesty and Rock of Ages, I pray that the dream of Prophet Isaiah concerning the time of cosmic reconciliation may come true for us: that wolves and sheep will live together in peace, and leopards will lie down with young goats...that cows and bear will eat together, and their calves and cubs will lie down in peace...that lions will eat straw as cattle do...and that even a baby will not be harmed if it plays near a poisonous snake. Yes, let Isaiah's jubilee dream be realised in our day that they shall hammer their swords into ploughshares, and their spears into pruning hooks. Let the dream of the Psalmist be fulfilled, that kindness and truth shall meet, and justice and peace shall kiss; that truth shall spring out of the earth, and justice look down from heaven.

As the Jubilee Year begins Wonderful Counsellor, help us to recognise that to have peace in the world we must first have peace in our hearts. Impress upon this generation the fact that we cannot shake hands with clenched fists. Yes, that just as we cannot get a rose through planting a noxious weed, we cannot have peace while harbouring hate in our hearts. Impress upon us the fact that the end does not justify the means, so good ends cannot justify immoral means. Disarm our hearts during this year of peace, Oh Lord, and free us from the violence of war, for war begins in the hearts of human beings. Let our hearts nurture peace and cultivate love instead of war. Help us to recognise like Thomas Merton that the God of peace is never glorified by human violence. Open our eyes to see that violence is a descending spiral, begetting the very thing it seeks to destroy, and destroying the very thing it claims to defend. Enable us to appreciate with Martin Luther King Jr. that darkness cannot drive out darkness, just as hate cannot drive out hate, and that returning violence for violence multiplies violence, adding deeper darkness to a night already devoid of stars. Help us to accept the words of Mahatma Gandhi that "counter hatred only increases the surface and depth of hatred."

Make us understand with Pope John Paul II that violence is the failure of all true humanism, that violence is a lie, for it goes against the truth of humanity, that violence is a grave crime against humanity, for it destroys the very fabric of human society, that violence only delays the day of justice, that violence destroys the work of justice, and that violence is the enemy of justice. Yes, help us Oh Lord to accept the truth that as a personal or social method, violence is totally incapable of changing anything. Make us heed the passionate call of the pope who recently had cause to say to the men and women of the world: "On my knees I beg you to turn away from the paths of violence and to return to the ways of peace."

Grant Oh Lord a heart of flesh to the men and women of my generation, that we may heed the prophetic call of this spiritual leader. Long before the era of John Paul II, Martin Luther King Jr. had reasoned that the choice today is no longer between violence and non-violence. He said "it is either non-violence or non-existence. Ah Lord, show the men and women of our age that the Christian teaching of indiscriminate love, embracing friend and so-called enemy, has become a practical necessity, for with the present level and dimension of violence, humanity is on the verge of committing suicide. Show us that the basic Christian teaching of unconditional love has become an imperative, in an age when indiscriminate destruction threatens the human community and the planet entrusted to its care.

Help us Lord through the twenty-first century to break the cycle of violence in the world and in our society. Teach us the unalterable law that hatred only ceases by love. Make the men and women of this and future generations know that the brave and the heroic are not those who can kill, oppress, dominate, and cause untold hardship. Make us know that the brave are those who can forgive, those who can love in return for hatred. Help us to see that it is in loving and forgiving those who tortured and killed him that Jesus revealed the full potential of humanity. Reveal to us the mystery of love which is the most subtle form of exorcism. Teach us the secret of your holy compassion that causes the devil so much distress.

Explain to us that there is a different way of responding to evil and to the machinations of our enemies that has the potential of breaking the endless cycle of retaliation that now threatens us all with ultimate violence. Show us the wisdom in the words of Pope John Paul II that no process of peace can ever begin unless an attitude of sincere forgiveness takes root in human hearts. Enable us to see with the Pope what an essential condition mutual forgiveness is in the journey towards authentic and lasting peace in the world and in our nation. And with James Forest, enable us to understand that the most remarkable miracle is not the transformation of water into wine, but the transformation of an enemy into a friend. Help us to see Lord how peace is the outcome of a sustained life of truth, justice, mercy, compassion, forgiveness, and human solidarity.

Make us understand, Oh Lord, that it is no use preaching peace unless we preach the things that make for peace. Help us to accept the wise words of Paul VI that if you want peace you must work for justice. Help us appreciate the words of John Paul II that respect for human rights is the secret of peace, and that the peace of all only comes from the justice of each. Enable those who seek peace to heed the words of Prophet Micah by acting justly, by loving tenderly, and by walking humbly before you Oh Lord. Let us remember that a society cannot live in peace with itself unless every human person is treated with dignity and all human life is reverenced as sacred. Help us realise that peace cannot be privatised, and that there is no room in this global village for pockets of peace amidst a world of poverty, oppression, violence, and strife. Show us clearly that it is not your will that in the same society some people should live in abject poverty while others lead a life of conspicuous consumption.

Enable us to know that all human beings are created in your image and likeness, and therefore each human person is inviolable. Impress upon us that "we are each responsible for all." Let us know that the fate of the politician threatened by the militant youth's bullet is the same as the fate of the destitute poor threatened by starvation. Make us recognise that the fate of the businessman violently harassed by hired assassins and Area Boys is the same as the fate of the condemned criminal awaiting public execution. Enable us to see that the fate of the innocent passenger threatened by the armed robber's gun is the same as the fate of the unborn child threatened by the abortionist's forceps. Help us to appreciate the words of Pope Paul VI that true human development is the advancement of the human person, the whole person, and all the people. Help us to recognise that the true measure of human civilisation is how the society takes care of the poor, the weak, the aged, the handicapped, and all those who are not "productive" in the narrow sense of the word.

Preach to us once again Oh God of mercy the Sermon on the Mount. Speak directly to our hearts and make us understand that powerful message of yours known as the Beatitudes. Spell out clearly for our comprehension the nine lessons that constitute the kernel of the Gospel. Help us to appreciate the fact that contrary to the general perception, the poor are truly blessed, the gentle are truly blessed, those who mourn are truly blessed, those who hunger and thirst for righteousness are truly blessed, the merciful are truly blessed, the pure in heart are truly blessed, the peacemakers are truly blessed, those persecuted in the cause of justice are truly blessed, and those abused and maligned for your sake are truly blessed. Make us understand the logic of the Magnificat, the song of Mary. Help us to see that the religion of Jesus Christ is not what Karl Marx called the opium of the people, but rather the most revolutionary instrument of social transformation. Help us to recognise Christianity as a force that exalts the lowly and casts down the proud, a force that feeds the hungry and sends the sated away empty. Impress on us the fact that Christ did not bring peace to the world as a kind of spiritual tranquilliser. Enable us to see with Thomas Merton that Christ brought to his disciples a vocation and a task - to struggle to establish peace not only in their own hearts but in the human society.

Reveal to us, Oh Lord, the mystery of the wilderness of compassion. Open our eyes to the secret of the desert of love. Enable us to overcome the widespread illusion that life is a property to be defended, that illusion which has given rise to so much violence. Instead, Lord, make us grasp the truth that life is a gift to be shared. Grant us the understanding which brings peace, and the peace which surpasses all understanding. Make us accept the fact that all pretensions to the contrary notwithstanding, only the meek and the humble shall inherit the earth, and that only the peacemakers shall be called sons and daughters of God. Yes, Lord, convince the men and women of this generation that all appearances to the contrary notwithstanding, peace will be the last word of history.

Let many of us be convinced of this so that we may not be afraid to take a chance on peace, that we may relentlessly work for peace in a world of strife, and that we may tirelessly teach peace amidst the deafening drums of war. Show us Lord how to take a stand amidst the pervading darkness in deliberate clarity, calmness, and confidence. Teach us how to be steadfast in perfect peace and cheerfulness, amid tension, gloom, selfishness, and hatefulness. Above all, Lord, help us to hold on to our ideals despite everything. Show us that we cannot build up our hopes on a foundation consisting of confusion, misery, and death. Show us that in a world of madness it is crazy to surrender our dreams, and to begin to see life as it is rather than as it should be. Help us to keep our hope for as long as we live, for as Dostoevsky says, to live without hope is to cease to live.

Pour out your Spirit from on high that right will dwell in the desert and justice will abide in the orchard, that justice will bring about peace, and right produce calm and security. We agree, Lord, that where there is no vision, the people do perish, that a nation without integrity cannot know peace. We accept that the fear of the Lord is the beginning of wisdom. And we know that unless the Lord builds a house, the labourers labour in vain. As you offer us a new opportunity to live life to the full in this Jubilee Year, make each one of us acknowledge that only you, God, can give authentic peace.

As the Jubilee Year 2000 begins, Father of all goodness, I ask you to visit Nigeria with your gentle spirit of repentance, conversion, forgiveness, reconciliation, and peace. Let your spirit of repentance and conversion pull down the mountains of hate and fill up the valleys of greed that are the principal obstacles to our national development. Let your spirit of forgiveness and reconciliation strike all vengeful hearts and like a divine shock therapy, heal the layers of resentment that are the cause of mutual acrimony and intermittent hostility in our land.

Look down upon us in the year 2000, Lord, and take us through the most pedagogical of pedagogues. Let the Nigerian political and economic elite understand the lessons of the last few years that were eaten by the locust. Let us come to realise that greed and avarice are a cancer which eats its own host to death; that lies, manipulation and political subterfuge have never, and will never nurture a people; that thievery, robbery, and roguery, by whatever name else it is called, when it becomes king in a land, that land rots; that when hooliganism and banditry get into high places, the superstructure soon comes crashing down; and that where lawlessness becomes the norm and illegality becomes the rule, the people soon perish.

Intervene in our affairs, Oh Master of the Universe and recreate the world for us. Pour out your Spirit from on high, that the desert may become an orchard, and the orchard be regarded as a forest. Look down from on high, Lord, that the winds of righteousness may blow from Sokoto to Kano, and that the waters of justice may flow from Lagos to Calabar. Visit this land this jubilee year Lord, that right may dwell on the highlands of Jos and Yola, and equity may flourish in the creeks of Warri and Yenagoa. Come and finish your work in our midst Oh God of compassion so that truth may reign on the rocks of Abuja and Abeokuta and love may grow on the hills of Enugu and Ibadan. Come and finish your good work in Nigeria, that peace may flourish on the plains of Makurdi, and Kaduna and that security may abide in the forest regions of Abakaliki and Benin City.

Breathe your powerful breath Oh Lord over the champions of our national destiny, until the lives of the lowly become precious in their eyes, and poverty and destitution are replaced by dignity and prosperity. Pour your oil of anointing on the administrators of the Nigerian commonwealth until the hungry are fed and the thirsty are given drink, and leadership becomes synonymous with shepherding. Let your justice roll like a rolling stone over the mountains of Adamawa and Taraba, and your peace flow like an overflowing stream in the valleys of Delta and Bayelsa. Confirm this jubilee year as the year of your favour, Oh God, that our land may be full of the knowledge of the Lord as the waters cover the seas.

Gracious God, we are embarking on a year-long holiday in the tradition of the biblical jubilee, to recuperate, to rejuvenate and to reciprocate your bounteous love. So let our land lie fallow throughout this sabbath of sabbaths, that we may recollect ourselves enough as to engage in a mission of reconciliation, offering and receiving forgiveness and proclaiming a general amnesty for offenders and transgressors, urging them to sin no more. Let our land lie fallow as we promulgate a moratorium on all anger and vengeance and announce a cessation of all oppression and exploitation. Let our land lie fallow as we celebrate the jubilee with a ceasefire between warring parties, urging them to sheath their swords and bury their dead along with their hatchets. Let the land lie fallow as we sound the trumpet throughout the land, proclaiming the liberty of all the people and the restoration of creation. Let the land lie fallow and lead our countrymen and women from death to life, from falsehood to truth, from despair to hope, from fear to trust, from hate to love, and from war to peace. Let the land lie fallow and fill our hearts, our families our country and our world with peace. Yes, Lord, let the land lie fallow as we hallow the 2000th birthday of Jesus Christ with a jubilee of thanksgiving, reconciliation, justice, and peace.

God of infinite goodness, if you will do all these for us, I pledge my total commitment to the biblical ethos of the jubilee. I pledge to put my entire life and all the resources you have bestowed upon me at the service of justice, reconciliation, and peace. I know that I cannot change anything in the world until I have been sufficiently transformed myself. So today and everyday that I may live, I pledge to say no to hate. I pledge to say no to ethnic bigotry or the idolatry of the tribe. I pledge to say no to greed and avarice. I pledge to say no to bribery and corruption in all its manifestations. I pledge to say no to religious intolerance. And I am committed to giving others the knowledge it takes to do the same.

If you will intervene in our affairs in the manner I have requested, and if you will do us these favours, I pledge that on my part I shall cry out against the various manifestations of the culture of death in our society. I shall cry out against the culture of abortion by which the life of the unborn child is cruelly terminated. I shall cry out against hired assassinations by which perceived enemies are callously eliminated. I shall cry out against capital punishment by which an entire society shamelessly celebrates vengeance. I shall cry out against jungle justice and extra-judicial killings at the hands of security agents. I shall cry out against mob justice or the summary execution of mere suspects by an angry mob. I shall repeat your injunction in the Decalogue, "thou shall not kill," to the men and women of my generation until my vocal cords collapse. Yes, Lord, I pledge not to compromise with violence, whether personal or social, national or international, for it is always wrong. And I pledge not to adjust to injustice, for to be well adjusted in a bad situation is not at all desirable.

I make these commitments, Lord, with the awareness that the end of life is not to achieve pleasure and avoid pain. I make these pledges because I recognise with Jesus that the end of life is to stand up for the truth of God, in season and out of season, welcome or unwelcome, come what may. I make these promises, Lord, because I know that it is only by giving our lives away that we truly find life, and that the truest act of courage, or the strongest act of humanity is to sacrifice oneself for others in a totally non-violent struggle for justice. Good Lord, I ask that you grant me the special grace you granted your saints and martyrs to match the wicked person's capacity to inflict suffering with my capacity to endure suffering. This at the end of the day is what it means to be human. So, Lord, help me to be truly human.

Finally, Lord, I would like to be an expert in the art of peace-making: pulling down the mountains of selfishness, and filling up the valleys of greed, cutting down the thorn bushes of hostility and raising up the lilies of hospitality, building bridges across the rivers of hate, and bringing together the fragments of disparate humanity. Make me an expert in peace-making: stitching torn nerves and mending broken bones, igniting the fire of charity, and fanning the flame of humanity, rocking the boat of vengeance, and sending to the sea the ship of reconciliation, destroying the myth of power and control, and laying the foundation for a civilisation of love.

Lord, since I desire peace like St. Francis of Assisi, permit me to end my Jubilee Year Peace Prayer with the prayer of that celebrated apostle of peace: Make me an instrument of your peace; where there is hatred, let me sow your love; where there is injury, your pardon Lord; and where there is doubt, true faith in you. Oh, Master grant that I may never seek, so much to be consoled as to console; to be understood as to understand; to be loved as to love with all my soul. Make me an instrument of your peace; where there is despair, let me give your hope; where there is darkness, only light; and where there is sadness, ever joy, for it is in giving that we receive. It is in pardoning that we are pardoned. It is in dying (to self) that we are born to eternal life. Amen.

CHAPTER FIVE

Nigeria: Neglect of the Common Good
(Written on February 8, 2000)

Ours is a country that is richly endowed by the Almighty God. Nigeria overflows with natural resources, from oil and gas to limestone and iron ore, we have them in plenty. Only recently, more offshore deposits of high-quality crude oil were discovered. The climate is conducive for rich agricultural production all year round. The weather is mild in most parts of the country. Added to these is the fact that our land has been spared the devastating floods, cyclones, earthquakes and volcanic eruptions that regularly plague some other parts of the world. And in terms of human resources, the country harbours a large and active population that includes talented people abundantly blessed with skills and abilities. So, by way of endowment, God placed Nigeria in a position not only to bring prosperity and well-being for its teeming population, but also respect from a world that appreciates God's goodness.

Yet Nigeria is today counted as one of the poorest countries in the world. Ignorance, poverty, malnutrition, disease and premature death, are the lot of many in our society. In spite of the enormous resources bestowed upon our land, social infrastructures in the form of portable water, decent housing, electricity, functional health and educational institutions, public transportation and telephone, etc., are beyond the reach of the generality of the people. And whereas the generality of the people live with multiple deprivations that amount to an affront on human dignity, a few smart Nigerians lead a lifestyle of conspicuous consumption.

A critical look at our recent history shows that the elite class in this country has been in large measure insensitive to the plight of the masses who look up to them for succour. As politicians, traditional rulers, military administrators, successful businessmen and women, and religious leaders, they have often neglected to do something about housing for the generality of the population, while they build monstrous mansions for themselves at various locations in the country. Some of these structures are unoccupied for years and left at the mercy of lizards and cockroaches. The leaders have often neglected to do something about public schools in Nigeria, while they send their children to exclusive private schools in Europe or America where they pay incredible amounts of money that would have been enough to turn things around in Nigeria. They have often neglected to do something about the dilapidated health institutions in the country as a result of which many poor Nigerians have died prematurely, yet these leaders patronise the best hospitals and clinics abroad, keeping themselves alive with the latest medical technology at very high costs.

Looking at the Nigerian socio-political and economic landscape, one can discern a near total neglect of the common good in the personal lifestyle, and in the value orientations, policies and projects, pursued by our leaders and the privileged few in our society. The common good is defined as the good of all in a society. It is the welfare of the whole community. The common good is the proper object of the just ordering of society. Human societies themselves exist to promote the common good. Governments exist to protect and defend the common good. Politicians are supposed to be elected to office only after they have demonstrated a special charism and passion for the furtherance of the common good. The Common Good is different from and superior to the good of any individual. Whereas individual good looks to the good of a single person or group, the common good is concerned about the good of the corporate body. The good of individuals and groups however sometimes coincide with the common good, but they should never be confused.

The idea of the common good is a fundamental plank of the Social Teachings of the Catholic Church. It is anchored on the Christian notion of the dignity of the human person, the human person who is created in the image and likeness of God. This dignity of every man and woman is understood by the Church to be as a result of the human person's divine origin, his or her supernatural end, and his or her transcendence. Also, the human person's happiness and ultimate fulfilment are only realisable in community. Thus, against the crass individualism upon which liberal or unbridled capitalism is sustained, the Church emphasises the universal destination of the goods of the earth, and the need for equity and fairness in the distribution of the resources of the earth. In the face of human greed that is sometimes expressed in the wholesale appropriation of all the land and mineral resources by a tiny few, the Church maintains that the goods of the earth are meant for the sustenance of all in the human society.

The truth of the universal destination of goods which the Church teaches is based on the biblical concept of the divine patrimony of the goods of the earth, as well as on the Christian idea of the human person's responsibility towards his or her neighbour. For a society to be truly human, individuals must consider the welfare of their neighbour as part of their responsibility. Thus, Pope Paul VI in the encyclical letter *Populorum Progressio,* describes development as "the advancement of the person, the whole person, and all the people." The right to life which the Church promotes assiduously also implies the right of all to minimum resources required for sustaining life. And in seeking the basic requirements for the sustenance of life, "we are each responsible for all." The common good therefore does not permit a situation where abject poverty will exist side by side with conspicuous consumption.

The Church recognises that individuals, families and groups have a right to acquire private property, in pursuit of their individual destiny, and for the enhancement of their comfort and their security, and in order to promote a healthy work ethic. This right to private property is however not absolute. It has a social mortgage. It is curtailed or checkmated by the good of the generality of the people. The common good is violated when an individual or group of individuals appropriate or amass for themselves an unreasonably high percentage of the earth's resources, while others are starved of the basic necessities of life. No matter how intelligent the individual may be, no one has the right to more than a fair share of the earth's resources, since they are destined for the good of all. A society where floating islands of wealth are to be found amidst a sea of degrading poverty cannot be said to be truly human.

The right to life which the 1948 United Nations Charter proclaims, implies also the right of all to minimum resources required for sustaining life. And in seeking the basic requirements for the sustenance of life, "we are each responsible for all." The common good therefore does not permit a situation where abject poverty will exist side-by-side with conspicuous consumption. The common good does not permit a situation whereby some people are able to buy private jets and drive around in the most expensive cars, when in the same society there are handicapped people who cannot be provided with wheelchairs or Braille materials.

Private property in the human society has a social mortgage. It is curtailed or checkmated by the good of the generality of the people. The common good is violated when an individual or group of individuals appropriate or amass for themselves an unreasonably high percentage of the earth's or the country's resources, while others are starved of the basic necessities of life. No matter how intelligent the individual may be, no matter how hardworking the individual may be, no one has the right to more than a fair share of the earth's resources, since they are destined for the good of all. A society where floating islands of wealth are to be found amidst a sea of degrading poverty cannot be said to be truly human.

Government exists in society to promote the common good, to ensure the best possible good for everyone, or at least for the highest possible number of people. This means that in order to promote the common good, human authorities must be constantly engaged in promulgating such laws or putting in place such juridical structures that will guarantee the right of individuals to private property, but also the juridical structures that will regulate and checkmate the acquisitive instinct of individuals. In this way governments will ensure just and equitable distribution of the resources of the land. It is the responsibility of government to protect the vulnerable poor from the excesses of the powerful rich who are often tempted to sell the poor for a pair of sandals. This role of government should hold particular attraction for Christians who appreciate the fact that the Lord Jesus Christ made a preferential option for the poor. That is to say that when there is a conflict between the rich and the poor, the Lord Jesus chooses to pitch his tent with the poor who are more vulnerable.

Thus, within the context of its teaching on the common good, the Church rejects both the crass individualism that is behind liberal capitalism, and the violation of individual rights and freedom that is implied in atheistic communism. Both systems are seen as an affront on the human person who is created in the image of God with freedom, and who must live in community with others and share resources with them.

Part of the challenge of the Church's teaching on the common good for present day Nigeria is that the privileged few should "live simply so that others may simply live." The criminal neglect of the common good by a succession of self-serving leaders is responsible in large measure for the widespread violence and social insecurity in the land. Today we have millions of unemployed and unemployable youths, ill-trained and ill-motivated. In every urban centre, these youths now constitute themselves into a dangerous mob that is ready to visit violence on their people at the slightest provocation. As they say, the fathers have eaten sour grapes, and the children's teeth are on edge.

Perhaps if our successive leaders were less selfish and self-seeking, the situation would have been different. Perhaps if they gave some thought to the common good in the management of our abundant national resources, the situation would have been different. For Nigeria to make true progress, the privileged few must develop a new sensitivity to the common good.

The privileged few must recognise that the goods of the earth belong to God, and that whatever they possess, they are only holding such goods in trust. They must recognise that they are merely stewards, who are bound to give an account of their stewardship one day.

We need to change our conception of leadership. We must begin to see leadership as stewardship and not an opportunity to exploit the people in every way for personal aggrandizement. It is time for us to re-examine our structures and undertake essential and far-reaching reformation to change the country's leadership profile for the better. Nigerians must painstakingly insist on good leaders, not mediocre functionaries, charlatans, thieves and brigands. The good leader is one who should be ready to make sacrifices for the sake of the common good. Those who aspire to leadership positions must have a sense of mission and vision. They must have a passion for the poor, the weak, the handicapped, and others on the margins of society.

Nigerians must be clear on what the good leader is not. The good leader is not the idle Nigerian politician who is in politics for the spoils of office, one whose only visible profession is politics and who has no other viable means of sustainable support. The good leader is not the feudalist ruler whose historical foundations, structured as they are on ignorance are antithetical to democratic principles. Feudalist authority structures are still very much around us. Those who perpetuate these structures often think nothing of holding down majority of the people in penury and serfdom, while feeding fat on the blood and tears of the very flock they are supposed to shepherd.

The Bible says that "where there is no vision, the people do perish." Nigeria as a corporate entity has been on the verge of collapse, due to the utter lack of vision on the part of its successive leaders, in the face of monumental corruption, structural injustice and falsehood in the body politic. The remnant of the Nigerian elite who are equipped with superior perception and have not joined the madding crowd, are challenged by the exigencies of today to quickly get to work, to analyse the situation on the ground in the light of the common good and to champion the cause of truth, reconciliation and wholesome economic and political development in our land. Even in an environment of widespread falsehood, political sycophancy, social injustice and economic profligacy, where what matters to many people are *brown envelopes* and *Ghana-must-go bags*, while the country goes up in flames, those with courage and fortitude among us must vehemently reject the so-called "Nigerian factor," and constantly present to our leaders and to the world at large, the vision of Nigeria as it ought to be run.

In an environment of widespread debauchery and mediocre leadership, those of us who are endowed with wisdom and vision must constantly resist the triumph of mediocrity and challenge the celebration of insanity in our land. We must not be caught in a conspiracy of silence while a hundred thousand lives are lost, and a hundred million dreams are damned in a conflagration that is contrived by the insatiable greed and lust for power of a few remnants of primitive feudalism. Therefore, truly wise Nigerians who know the cause-and-effect relationship between the economic profligacy and political brinkmanship of a few prostitutes of power and the increasing pauperization or destitution of the masses of the people, must not look on passively while these pallbearers of a lost generation domesticate our commonweal and turn our land to ruins.

Thus, the challenge before Nigerians is how to develop a new sense of national cohesion, a new sense of patriotism, and a new sense of the common good. We must get to work and develop for ourselves a new vision and civilisation that will change pretentious leaders into true stewards of the people. For unless and until we come by this new vision and civilisation, by which greed, avarice, corruption, hatred, primitive feudalism and the manipulation and exploitation of religion and ethnicity are destroyed, the Nigerian nation will yet remain distressed, and its people traumatised. I challenge you all to be torchbearers in the search for this new vision and civilisation for Nigeria. And may the Lord bless your little efforts with success.

CHAPTER SIX

Transforming our Prisons to Correctional Centres
(Written on July 17, 2000)

S unday July 9, 2000 was observed throughout the Catholic world as the Jubilee of Prisoners. Pope John Paul II celebrated Mass for the inmates at the central prison in Rome, while Bishops and priests were to do the same in their various territories, as a practical demonstration of jubilee solidarity. They were expected to preach to prisoners the message of God's love and mercy, especially towards those who have fallen to the margins of the human society. The Christian faithful were urged to use that occasion to show solidarity with prisoners through concrete acts of love and generosity. The entire society was called upon to see the jubilee of prisoners as an occasion in which they reflect on the condition of our prisons to see whether they are truly places for reformation and rehabilitation rather than chambers of torture. The jubilee presented an occasion for our society to take wide-ranging steps towards improving prison conditions to meet the requirements of elementary human rights, dignity and decency, and to fulfil the requirements of Christ's civilisation of love.

The plight of the Nigerian citizen unlucky enough to be a guest of a long-bastardised justice and penal systems is indeed a terrible one. Whether he is a lowly citizen or a highflier, a habitual criminal or social agitator, a swindler, rogue leader or drug peddler, whether he is an arsonist or assassin, a religious fanatic or armed robber, a rapist, abortionist or member of the nation's cult culture, those who end up in the bowels of those gulags we call prisons, invariably begin their descent into the valley of torture, deprivation and desperation. And here lies the challenge of the jubilee which proclaims forgiveness of debts, amnesty for offenders, freedom for captives and the merciful God's year of favour. The jubilee of prisoners should confront our pernicious prison culture and enkindle hope for the Nigerian prisoner.

The typical Nigerian prison is a hellhole conceptualised decades ago in colonial times when imprisonment was principally a tool in the hands of the occupation force that was meant to beat the restive elements in the conquered population into submission. Imprisonment under the colonial "masters" and their indigenous collaborators was characterised by widespread abuse, torture, starvation, and the cultivation of infectious skin diseases and tuberculosis. After nearly forty years of independence, the Nigerian prison system has not undergone any major transformation by way of making it a place for the correction, reformation and rehabilitation of the offender. Rather, from Gusau to Abakaliki, and from Kuje to Kirikiri, the facilities are designed to remind the offender daily of the punitive rewards of his confinement.

Overcrowding in Nigerian prisons and detention centres is legendary, just as are the attendant health hazards. The physical appearance of prisoners speaks volumes for prison accommodation and diet. There seems to be the generally accepted belief among our countrymen and women that the offender is beyond reform, that the guilt complex is a cloak he must wear for the rest of his life and that society can never again derive anything positive from him. Prison life devalues the convict's self-esteem, as he loses all hope of ever again returning to society a wholesome human person. At the end of his prison term, the ex-convict in our society is often totally disillusioned and in despair. With nothing more to lose the angry victim of a callous penal system often slides deeper into crime in a bid to get even with the society that has shaped his new image. Violence as they say begets further violence. At the end of the day both the prisoner and the society that holds him captive, gain nothing from the experience of imprisonment. And the self-righteous segment of society which prides itself on being decent and law-abiding, nevertheless fails to measure up to the true test of human development and human civilisation, which is said to be "how the society treats its weakest and most vulnerable members." Thus, while on the part of the offender prison sentence under dehumanising conditions may mean the onset of despair, for the vengeful society which has put him away, it is the death of morality.

Central to the issue of prison rehabilitation is the social responsibility of the free society to its convicted brethren, in and out of captivity. The rehabilitation should begin at the moment of conviction and should be sustained until the stigma of social rejection is removed and the ex-convict attains emotional stability, spiritual equilibrium, economic independence, and social integration. This calls for a totally new orientation in our justice and penal system. It calls for a re-conception of the aims and objectives of our prisons and detention centres, and a review of the structures that make imprisonment such a harrowing experience. The embarrassingly dehumanising juridical and physical structures relating to prisoners in our country today are in large measure a consequence of a primitive notion of crime and the criminal, and what we understand as the purpose of punishment.

If we are to witness a major change in the conduct of our prisons and detention centres, and in the treatment of those who have fallen foul of our social norms and ethos; if we are to achieve a reasonable degree of transformation and rehabilitation on the part of ex-convicts, with a low degree of recidivism; if we are to achieve all these, what we require is a moral and spiritual revolution - a transformation on the level of our individual and national psyche. We require a radical change in our notion of imprisonment as a purely punitive, vengeful and vindictive measure, which only succeeds in making hardened criminals out of first offenders, to one that is meant to correct, reform and rehabilitate the offender, so that he may return to the society better disposed to contribute his unique talents to the development of society.

We require a new orientation in the development and maintenance of prison structures, both physical and administrative or juridical. At the level of juridical structures, the state can do a lot to put a human face to the fate of convicts. These include the review of detention and prison rules, experimentation on the parole system, and the provision of free and adequate defense of felons. Each prison needs to have an adequate health facility to respond swiftly to the health needs of the inmates. Where a well-equipped clinic with a doctor is not available, the prison should have a stand-by vehicle to convey sick members to the nearest hospital. And to enhance the physical and mental health of the prisoners, adequate recreational facilities must be put in place in each prison, and time must be given for each prisoner to exercise himself or herself. Even those said to be in solitary confinement need to be allowed some time for physical recreation, unless their sentence is "death by instalments."

Christian leaders must count it as a constitutive dimension of their missionary enterprise to give hope and joy to those in prison, for they are counted among the poor - the little ones for whom Jesus Christ has so much affection, and for whose welfare he demonstrated such passionate commitment. It is in this way that we shall nurture hope, and make it endure in the experience of "the dark night" of our prisons and detention centres. The good news must be continually preached to and celebrated with our prisoners, detainees, and ex-convicts that God loves the world so much that he made out of his only son a healing balm to soothe the wounds of ailing humanity. Prisoners, detainees and ex-convicts in our country need to hear it said, but also, they need to witness the practical celebration of the truth that God loves the world so much that he sent his son *not to judge the world*, but to save it. Yes, they need to witness the celebration of those comforting words of the Psalmist that "If you Oh Lord should mark our guilt, Lord, who would survive? But with you is found forgiveness, and for this we revere you." They need to witness the regular celebration of the words of Matthew 25:31-46 "...when I was in prison, you came to visit me." This is the way to conquer despair and enkindle hope in the distressed prisoners, detainees and ex-convicts in this country, and the jubilee year is an auspicious time to do this.

CHAPTER SEVEN

NIGER DELTA: Our Guilt and Shame
(Written on December 17, 2000)

In less than two years after the Jesse incident, another fire disaster arising from burst petrol pipelines has occurred in the Niger Delta, claiming no less than 200 lives, most of them allegedly school children. Once again it is the poorest of the poor in the Niger Delta that have to pay the price for the ostentatious life of the rich few who are safely quartered in the Victoria Island area of Lagos or the exclusive area of Abuja.

In the last few years, the poor people of the Niger Delta have taken more than their fair share of the consequences of the political profligacy and economic debauchery of the Nigerian leadership. The Niger Delta has been the victim of a callous environmental exploitation and abuse in the form of gas flaring, crude oil spillage, and explosion from burst petrol pipes. The Niger Delta region has lost valuable farmlands and fishing waters. The region has lost thousands of able-bodied young men and women in the numerous poverty-propelled violent conflicts that have taken place there in the last few years. Ogoni, Andoni, Eleme and Okrika, are war-ravaged towns. The Ijaw, the Itsekiri, the Urhobo and the Ilaje are constantly at each other's throat over such matters as the citing of Local Government Headquarters. While villages like Jesse and Egborode were reduced to desert lands by gas explosions, others like Odi have been brought down to ruins by over-zealous security agencies who showed the world that they were ready to sacrifice any number of human beings in order to protect the oil reserves located in those areas.

Much of the land itself remains a tale of neglect and abuse. For after nearly forty years of oil exploration and exploitation in the Niger Delta, there is no pipe borne water in most of the villages; there is no electricity in most of the villages; there are no paved roads in most of the villages; there are no modern health facilities in most of the villages. The majority of the people are still living in squalor. Yet a sizeable amount of the resources used to build the flyovers and skyscrapers in Lagos, Abuja,

Kaduna, Kano, Jos, Ibadan, Enugu, and Benin, come from the ancestral land of the Niger Delta people. In the last thirty years or so the Nigerian economy has depended almost wholly on the money generated from the black gold found in the Niger Delta. Nigerian oil barons have built palaces for themselves that would compete with royal mansions anywhere in the world. Some of them have private jets, while others ride some of the most expensive cars in the world. Perhaps these oil dealers and contractors consider themselves smart. Indeed, they are. But at what cost? What price is being paid for their smartness?

In the last few years of debauchery, billions of dollars' worth of oil money was callously looted out of this country by leaders who should be certified clinically mad. If a thorough probe should be conducted into the financial dealings of all senior government functionaries during the kleptocratic dispensations of Babangida and Abacha, and if justice must be done, a number of those flaunting their ill-gotten riches before our eyes today may be remanded in prison or sent to the asylum. But that is not all. What about the rest of Nigeria, particularly the elite? What have we done? What have we failed to do? What could we have done that we neglected to do? Can we truly watch the plight of the Niger Delta people without a profound sense of guilt and shame?

After the last fire disaster, many Nigerians expressed outrage at the behaviour of those young people who went with plates and pans, and buckets and pots to scoop petrol from leaking pipes and perished in the process. Someone even came on TV to say, *"good for them, God don catch them."* But this kind of judgement results from a jaundiced analysis of the situation on the ground. Those who make this kind of judgement do not appreciate the dynamics of poverty. They do not know that poverty has its own culture, and that extreme poverty humiliates and degrades people to the extent that they lose a good amount of their reasonability. What the self-righteous commentators on the fire explosions do not seem to understand is that the acrimonious poverty in Nigeria today, makes human life so cheap that it can readily be exchanged for a bucket of petrol.

Indeed, what many comfortable observers of the situation do not appreciate is that the impoverishment and abuse of the people of Nigeria is the primary violence in the land. All other instances of violence, including the actions that culminated in the fire explosions at Jesse and Egborode constitute only a secondary violence. Why should anyone in

Nigeria (and in the rich Niger Delta for that matter) be so poor that he or she has to go with pots and pans to scoop petrol from leaking pipes in order to survive? With a land so rich in natural resources including petroleum, why should anyone have to buy gasoline, kerosine or diesel oil in plastic containers? If petrol and diesel were readily available in gas stations as they should be, would any driver stop to buy the same products from those hawking them with pots, pans, buckets and basins? Those who make thoughtless comments about the violence, the fires, and the regular tension in the Niger Delta need to think again.

The truth which many are running away from is that the successive leaders of this country have committed genocide against the Niger Delta people. Each time we put on our TV and watch those fires blazing, with those poverty-stricken children roasting in them, let the rich and powerful among us who have got more than their fair share of the benefits of the Niger Delta oil be filled with guilt and shame, for they are beneficiaries of the callous despoliation of a people. Yes, each time we hear reports of hundreds of deaths in one or the other of those poverty-provoked communal clashes in the Niger Delta, let the wealthy and comfortable among us who are protected by high walls and iron bars in their Lagos, Abuja or Kano villas, be filled with guilt and shame, for they feed fat on the human lives that were recklessly wasted in the Niger Delta. Yes, the Niger Delta is what it is today because of the combined forces of corruption, greed, neglect, and abuse.

I believe that the blood of the poor children sacrificed in the Niger Delta continuously cries out to heaven. And we must do something immediately to redress the anomaly. The country is in deep trouble. For all of us it can no longer be business as usual. The fire explosions in Jesse and Egborode are only a metaphor for our national predicament. The president must be told to sit up and face the challenges on the ground rather than junketing round the world. The legislators too must be told to abandon their accustomed game of mischief and intrigue and answer the call of the moment. The entire nation must now be urgently engaged in the process of restitution, reconstruction and reconciliation with regard to the Niger Delta, if more devastating fires are not to occur.

CHAPTER EIGHT

Where is our Sanity?
(Written on September 28, 2001)

Ours is a haven of incredulity. Nigeria does not fail to confound even the most casual of observers of our special brand of polity and democratic evolution. Whether it is our tragicomic national show of political shenanigans in governance or the circus sideshow involving our untouchable ex-heads of state and the Oputa Human Rights Violation Commission, Nigeria does not fail to confound. But today I am indeed horrified, extremely outraged and thoroughly shamed by the reprehensible fare of blind hate, of criminal intolerance and bloodletting we now serve to the world as our own version of crime against humanity.

As America experienced the height of international terrorism with the shock attacks of September 11, here at home, our Jos, the perch of peace and tolerant living, the self-styled land of peace and haven of hospitality, was rocked by an unprecedented measure of hate killings among residents. All that reputation of Jos went up in smoke as the once sedate and shining tin city was drenched in human blood and charred by the burning remains of homes, goods and prayer houses.

After Jos, came Kano, the perennial hotbed of religious fundamentalism and social upheaval. Kano, that prides itself as the commercial nerve centre of Nigeria's hinterland, but one whose execution of organised terror and mayhem against non-indigenes and non-Muslims is legendary. Kano, said to be the rallying point for imported alien tribes recruited from time to time from neighbouring states to perpetrate anarchy and chaos. It was the turn of Kano as usual to lead Nigeria's fundamentalism in orchestrating support for Osama bin Laden in faraway Afghanistan. Hundreds of our citizens again had to die and countless costs in losses by arson and looting had to be borne for a cause that is as opaque and senseless as it is intrusive and unjust.

And hot on the heels of Kano came the festering Tiv/Jukun communal antipathy, escalating once again into an explosive discharge of intemperate fury in bloody skirmishes and killings. And utterly despicable and condemnable is the alleged abduction, killing and decapitation of 19 soldiers said to be on a peace mission to the area. And in these traumatic scenarios, the reactive response of our governments is entirely predictable. The leaders normally take their time reacting to potentially destabilising developments as and when they occur. They hardly take steps to checkmate or neutralise crises and conflicts. So, they repeat themselves.

With these bloody events happening in tandem, I found myself wondering, like a man in a stupor, if it was all for real, or if I was suffering some kind of nightmare. Was I being harassed and tormented by some evil force playing these gory scenes across my subconscious? Would I wake from the anguish and mental agony, or was I the victim of some unremitting hallucination?

Then suddenly I was jarred into full wakefulness by the horror and incomprehension of what can only be described as the officially sponsored massacre of unarmed and non-belligerent villagers, primitive style, in the name of revenge for the killing of the 19 soldiers by yet to be identified criminals of the Tiv/Jukun fracas that snuffed out the lives of over 200 people. But then, the heavy overkill demonstrated by soldiers in Tiv land suggests that their own kind are a step above the law and natural justice and so the law can be set aside for them to mete out their own instant jungle justice. Any wonder therefore that the method, dimension and intensity of the Benue carnage, said to be so outrageous, provoked widespread demonstrations by youths and students in the capital city of Makurdi. Should Nigerians not wonder therefore and ask themselves if they are not living under an illusion that they are indeed true citizens of a country committed to freedom and justice under the law?

Today, along with Afghanistan, Nigeria now features prominently on CNN and BBC as a place of vengeance, violence and war, a land of blood and tears. Today with the evidence of pain and death everywhere, I am filled with shame for my country Nigeria, that has been turned into one vast wasteland of strife with pockets of refugee camps harboring Nigerian citizens. Today I am filled with outrage against our leaders who have the prime duty of giving protection to life and property, but who connive in the trading of death and pretend to be in control. Today, I am awash with outrage against the leadership of Nigeria which sits back and gives off an air of well-being, when thousands of Nigerians are being regularly killed in ethnic and religious conflicts, and in peace time.

While the nation reels under the reverberations of our self-destructive expeditions in death, a silent form of terrorism has returned to haunt our homes. Adulterated kerosine has once again heralded its explosive presence in Lagos and elsewhere, scorching and incinerating many to death and spreading pain and grief. Can we ever rid ourselves and our country of the greed, the indiscipline and the moral decadence that promote such crimes against the public? Is ours indeed a nation without a soul?

I am deep in disgust at the fact that Nigerians seem to have lost the sense of shame and remain impervious to the damage effect on their common psyche. I am filled with indignation that my countrymen and women seem to have lost the sense of outrage for they seem to regard these happenings as mere items of news. I am stunned with shock at my countrymen and women whose emotions have become so deadened that they can only but gloat over these gory tales.

As the country is convulsed by these traumatic episodes in quick succession, I am propelled by righteous indignation at our leaders who seem to see no merit in declaring a period of national mourning. I am appalled at the insensate statements by some of our leaders and their rush to judgement, justifying some of these events. I am assailed by disgust at the unsavoury manner of (graphic) coverage of these events by some elements of the mass media. For it looks to me more like returning to the primitive days of gladiators and bloody pastimes.

Where these gory events should provoke demonstrable identification with our brutalized sensibilities, our leaders seem more concerned with manipulations of their parties and constituencies for their re-election. They seem more concerned about electoral bills that may favour or threaten their individual selfish agendas. Where these events should prompt pre-emptive steps and concrete remedial measures to alleviate physical and mental suffering, our leaders seem satisfied with living the lie. A major part of our national problems is constituted by our leadership whose ineptitude and culpability in moments of crises, compound our national structural predicament. This is why regrettably, our future as a cohesive whole, as a united nation with viable and dependable social structures remains entrapped in the dark tunnel of national disorder.

Where is our sense of sanity in this season of madness when reason, good sense and common interest seem to have taken leave of us? Where is our compassion and where is our respect for the sacredness of human blood when we have turned our country into one vast slaughterhouse and turned on our own kind in merciless self-destruction? Where lie the dignity, the sanctity and inviolability of human life in our national landscape, littered as it is with decapitated corpses and burnt-out homes and property, when we feign knowledge of God and his punishment, and pretend that we have any modicum of national security?

When some thirteen years ago I embarked on research work on an African Christian Humanism, I drew copiously on what I perceived as the rich heritage of Africa's humanistic tradition. I needed to set on record the well-known fact of African reverence for life, and the established reputation of our forebears for sympathy, kindness, respect, love, regard for the stranger, communal cohesion, family ties and deference to seniority and authority. I needed to set all these against the impersonal Western values evolving today. Now after Odi, Kaduna, Sagamu, Ife/Modakeke, Umuleri/Aguleri, Lagos, Nasarawa, Tafawa Balewa, Jos, Zakibiam, Makurdi and countless other trouble spots, I am put to shame - my assertions unable to stand up to any serious scrutiny.

For a country that has been repeatedly and brutally violated, what a wretched fate I have living in Nigeria at this time. Yet, like every other Nigerian citizen, I have no other country but this one. How I wish to God that in this hour of despondency Nigeria will rediscover its soul and that Nigerians will find the faith to turn the country away from self-destruction. Oh, how I wish...

CHAPTER NINE

Abuse of National Honours and Chieftaincy Titles
(Written on January 17, 2002)

Towards the end of last year, the government of Olusegun Obasanjo decorated 340 Nigerians with National Honours and Awards of various designations in a flashy ceremony that is typical of the Nigerian penchant for vainglory. The list was dominated by past leaders, both military and civilian. Of course, there was a sprinkling of personalities from the academia and the professions who are said to have distinguished themselves in their calling.

The recognition of 340 distinguished men and women among the Nigerian political, economic and academic elite would have been quite in order if we were not living in a pervasive environment of national distress. Such an event would have been a good thing if we truly had grounds for awarding merit and not mediocrity, if we had grounds for honouring service and not betrayal, and if we had grounds for celebrating progress and not inertia. From whichever way we wish to view Nigeria, there is a general consensus that all is not well with us today, and all has not been well for decades. By our own admission there is no shortage of dubious elements always on hand to muscle in on national matters, to derail and collapse national goals and processes, and to actively invest in state failure. Our national firmament remains a poor reflection of cohesion, unity, strength, industry, probity, discipline and patriotism, orderliness, – the very virtues for which honours are earned and bestowed in other climes.

Much of the pain, suffering and trauma in the land today is an accumulation of the monumental betrayal and failure of the Nigerian elite who have been involved in leadership at all levels. If these Nigerians were truly meritorious and deserving of the honours and titles that are being conferred on them, then we would not be where we are today. Their performance records should have reflected and resonated in all segments of our national life, and Nigeria would have been a better place to live in. If only we could think of a national roll of dishonour, and include in the list all who have not performed well as Heads of State, Governors, Military Administrators, Ministers, Commissioners, Special Advisers, Permanent Secretaries, Directors General, Managing Directors, General Managers, Local Government Chairmen and Councilors, etc., how many of our so-called meritorious Nigerians would escape such a list of dishonour?

What justification do we have to decorate so many elements of the Nigerian elite with the highest honours conceivable, when our nation is in a state of anomie? Can we truly take these awards in good conscience when the larger portion of the Nigerian landscape is engulfed in an atmosphere of angst and debilitating poverty? Are our leaders, past and present comfortable in applauding and celebrating merit awards when the fruits of our nationhood are as yet a mirage? Will the awards we have now conferred on past and serving functionaries of the state reverse the current miserable conditions of the masses? Will these awards heal the national wounds and cure the multiple woes of the land?

This is not to belittle the heroic efforts of a number of award recipients. There are indeed a number of people in the list who are high profile achievers and whose contributions to the nation are spectacular. But there are many in the list who may have no business being there. There are many in the list whose motivational drive is anything but patriotic or national. And it is not only those in and out of national limelight that merit recognition. Those in our midst who strive to give succour to the poorest of the poor are the ones who merit our nation's gratitude, not the greedy elite whose inordinate ambition for power and craze for money have reduced our country to such a pitiable state. Those Nigerians whose hunger for truth and passion for justice have forced them to make enormous sacrifices for our country, are the ones who deserve our national honours, not the political opportunists and prostitutes of power whose shameless deals have put our land through such a nightmare.

Those who held on tenaciously to the higher values of honesty, accountability, hard work and diligence, and who suffered impoverishment and social alienation through a period of widespread corruption and political profligacy, are the ones who truly should be given the highest recognition of our land, not the sycophants who sold Nigeria and its future to the late General Abacha and his deranged collaborators. Military officers, traditional rulers, political contractors, and others, cocooned in a life of comfort and conspicuous consumption, and far removed from the harsh realities of our rural communities and city slums and ghettos, can hardly lay claim to any merit or honour in a land so callously abused by a succession of self-serving leaders.

True, the acquisition and conferment of merit awards, chieftaincy titles, and honorary degrees to people with questionable character, is one of Nigeria's social problems that is fast turning into a national malaise. In fact, the phenomenon has reached such a nauseating extent that one wonders if the various individuals and institutions involved in this enterprise ever reflect on the effect the awards, titles and honours have on our society that is long traumatized by poor, ineffective and immoral leadership.

Traditional titles used to be a symbol of deserved recognition, a stamp of authority, an acknowledgement of moral leadership, a testimony to sterling qualities, and a proof of honour, achievement and service in the community. But how deserving are those who trade in chieftaincy titles in Nigeria today? Traditional rulers who confer these titles seem to be in the lead in bastardizing these titles, as the standard parameters for social relevance and qualification are no longer respected. Chieftaincy titles are now known to be selectively available on auction - to the highest bidder. It is no longer relevant if the potential recipient is a crook or a bandit. Of particular concern are serving officers of government who seek after or who are sought after for the conferment of chieftaincy titles. Is it not the height of impropriety for a government officer under whatever pressure to succumb to the immoral expedience of accepting a chieftaincy title while still serving? Good sense suggests that a title taken after service is over, when one's contributions to society have been exposed to public glare and found above board, carries more honour.

Today there is stiff competition in the academia to seek out prominent figures in government and society for the award of honorary degrees. It does not seem to matter whether the prominence of these people is founded on illegitimacy or political obfuscation. It equally does not seem to matter if the recipient is totally ignorant of the value and discipline of the award. What seems to matter are the avenues for reciprocal compensation which these awards create. All these aggregate to an indictment of the entire elite of the country, an elite that sees nothing wrong in the failure of the ruling class and the celebration of titles in a state of distress. It is an indictment of a fun loving and ego massaging leadership elite that will exploit to the last, the already impoverished masses of the land.

Some of the Nigerians being decorated and honoured these days may well be winners on the individual level, but collectively we are all part of a national team in a losing game of nation-building. As a group we are in for a long haul if we must redeem our nation and end the game on a winning note. The game is a long way from being over. Only if and when that happens can we truly recognise and celebrate those of our numbers who have distinguished themselves in bringing about a rejuvenation. Until then, public officers who are hungry for chieftaincy titles should first be concerned about their personal track records and the performance profile of the government in which they serve. Until then, they should be concerned about the social and economic structures they inherit, those that they initiate and those that they sustain. Until then, they should agonize over the impact of their policies on the living conditions of the masses they govern and determine whether their decisions put more food on the people's tables or smiles on their faces. Until then, we should keep our awards and honour our heroes in due time, posthumously if need be.

CHAPTER TEN

The Sharia and Religious Persecution in Nigeria
(Written on January 25, 2002)

Introductory Remarks

I congratulate the National Council of Women Religious for this National Day celebration and for choosing such a topic for your reflection. I am indeed gratified to know that you as Women Religious in Nigeria are beginning to study such issues as the *Sharia*, thus abandoning the attitude and disposition of passivity or apathy with regard to matters of social concern and are taking your rightful place as enlightened citizens of Nigeria, who should use your privileged positions in the Nigerian society to advance the cause of truth, equity, justice, national reconciliation, social development and peace. Perhaps your involvement in the *Sharia* discourse has become an imperative today, after we all have seen with the Taliban regime of Afghanistan and the death sentence passed on lady Safiya of Sokoto, how horrible the plight of women could be under a strict *Sharia* legal system.

I have decided to formulate the topic of this reflection as: *The Sharia and the phenomenon of religious persecution in Nigeria*, recognising from the outset that the greatest implication of the imposition of the *Sharia* legal system in some states of our country is the intensification and transformation into official state policy, what we have always known as religious persecution in the Northern part of Nigeria. Before the *Sharia* became state law in Zamfara and the other states, religious persecution was often not blatant but subtle, and what sometimes camouflaged as religious violence in the North was often the cumulative result of a complexity of interlocking factors, including failure in the socio-economic and political structures of our society, involving real and perceived injustices, widespread poverty, large-scale youth unemployment, and the resultant resentment, anger, crime and violence. I believe that any sincere reflection on the Sharia and its implications on the society today must take these complex realities into consideration.

Muslims say that Islam is not just a religion, but a way of life. The *Sharia* is the legal system, which governs Islamic way of life. Unlike the code of Canon Law which restricts itself to religious and ecclesiastical matters, the *Sharia* is a comprehensive system of laws and regulations, injunctions and prescriptions, that is in a way equivalent to a nation's constitution and covering every aspect of the life of those in the particular society where the legal system is in force. Muslims often do not recognise what Christians and those with Western orientation call a distinction between Church and State. For the protagonists of the *Sharia,* there is no distinction between religion, politics and culture. These hard line Muslims, like their Jewish counterparts will see all aspects of human life, individual, social, economic and political as belonging to God and must be governed by what they understand to be God's law. That is why they regard the implementation of the Islamic legal system as part of their fundamental human rights, and not as a privilege. This orientation that sustains the Sharia order may well have worked well in primitive societies, characterised as they were by ignorance, uniformity, authoritarianism and superstition. But within the context of our post-enlightenment pluralistic and democratic societies, the *Sharia* has become an anachronism.

The Catholic Bishops' Conference of Nigeria has always made its stand on the *Sharia* issue very clear. Upholding the secular status of Nigeria, the Bishops have consistently warned the government and people of Nigeria about the evil consequences that will arise when the Islamic legal system is imposed on any state of Nigeria, for that would amount to elevating Islam to a state religion, thus violating section 10 of the 1999 Constitution which provides for the secularity of the country and governmental neutrality in matters of religion. At the September 2001 meeting of their Conference, the Bishops expressed their concern in the following terms:

> We are particularly concerned about the persistence of *Sharia*-related politics in the country. The adoption of the *Sharia* by some states in Nigeria has continued to create a situation of unrest in which people are killed and maimed, and thousands of others are displaced from their homes and places of work. ...many indigenes of the states concerned continue to suffer in silence because they cannot defend their rights and have nowhere to relocate to.

> We have repeatedly warned that the adoption of the *Sharia* as state law and extension of its scope are a flagrant violation of human rights of non-

Muslims in a multi-religious society and a secular state like Nigeria. We consider it an act of gross irresponsibility on the part of some officials – who are elected to defend the constitutional rights of every Nigerian to live anywhere without being discriminated against on the basis of religion or ethnicity – to use religion as a tool to advance their selfish interests and to foment violence among people. We urge all our leaders to refrain from making inflammatory statements that could further aggravate the situation of unrest in Nigeria.

We have warned earlier that the adoption of the *Sharia* as state law would infringe on the rights of non-Muslims; the reality on the ground has proved us right. We are shocked that the various arms of Government at Federal and State levels have remained indifferent to this problem which could bring disastrous consequences on our nation. It is wishful thinking for government to continue to believe that the *Sharia* problem will fizzle out with time. We warn that it is too costly to create a situation in which the destiny of this nation is left in the hands of fanatics, be they religious or political. Given the explosive nature of religious conflicts as evidenced in other parts of the world, we demand that the Federal Government acts decisively to uphold and defend the legitimate constitutional rights of all Nigerians.

The world of the 20th Century has witnessed enormous progress in the arts and sciences and in politics and religion. New norms of governance have emerged in our day to replace primitive legal modes that thrived on a regime of fear. There is greater recognition today of the place of the individual human person and the need to respect his or her dignity and freedom of conscience. In fact, respect for what have come to be known as fundamental human rights, has become the basis of the legitimacy of a governmental process. After the first and second world wars, which claimed over thirty million lives, the world woke up to the need to find a concrete basis for guaranteeing the rights of citizens. The high mark of this was the inauguration of the League of Nations which later metamorphosed into the United Nations in 1948.

The articulation and documentation of the United Nations' Declaration of Human Rights in 1948 provided the framework for the subsequent development of guidelines for ensuring that all its signatories use the guarantee and respect of human rights as a basis for the legitimacy of governments. With these developments, many social injustices hitherto taken for granted are no longer tolerable. From the abolition movement to the campaign for de-colonisation, and from the women liberation movement to the now widespread campaign for a sustainable natural environment, men and women are beginning to speak of one another in terms of a common brotherhood, and of the earth as the common patrimony, not only for all generations of humanity, past, present and future, but also of all living things.

The Historical Origins of the Sharia and Religious Persecution in Nigeria

The controversy over the *Sharia* law and the subtle or at times blatant acts of discrimination or persecution of non-Muslims in Nigeria, can be traced back to the political strategies of the British colonial administration in Nigeria. Long before the arrival of the British economic and political adventurists and explorers, Islam had made inroads into, and even established city-states in the North-eastern flanks of today's Nigeria. Some writers claim that this is as far back as the 11th Century. By 1804, the Sokoto Caliphate was established by Uthman dan Fodio. However, towards the end of the 19th Century, the British intensified their economic and political explorations and expeditions around the Niger, and by 1903 they conquered the Sokoto Caliphate.

When Christian missionaries followed up the British conquest into the southern parts of Nigeria, they came along with western education and the Christian faith. However, the experiences of the British with the products of western education was problematic. These educated Nigerians were the first to challenge British colonialism, an act that was considered more than just belligerent. The British reacted by cordoning off parts of the North that were coterminus with the boundaries of the crumbled caliphate. Among other things, their poor economy attracted them to the slave-holding feudal system which the caliphate had established. In the caliphate, slave status was ascribed to non-Muslims since the caliphate existed to further consolidate the home of Islam. The British were enamoured with the feudal system because, founded on the principles of Islam, it had an approach to life that was marked by a fatalistic submission to the will of God. This religious disposition resonated fast among a largely illiterate and poor population who accepted their social conditions largely as the will of God and were therefore unwilling to change the status quo.

The British, for their own selfish reasons therefore accepted to sign a pact with the caliphate to ensure that Christian missionaries were not allowed into the Muslim areas. This pact, known as the Pact of Non-Interference, ensured that the British did not allow Christian missionaries to come to preach in the Muslim areas. Even when Southern Christians moved to the North as skilled workers (due to their western education) or traders, their right of worship was circumscribed. To deal with the problem, the British designed a legal framework that consigned Christians to remote parts or outside the main cities. These settlements became known as *Sabon Gari* (new town) and they dotted all the major Muslim cities of the North. They were disparagingly referred to as areas where alcohol could be consumed and where prostitution could thrive. What is meant in effect was that all the Muslims who wanted to sin, were free to go to the *Sabon Gari*. In this way, the image of Christianity as an inferior religion which tolerated sin began to emerge in a rather surreptitious way.

Thus here, in these structures of discrimination, the seed of today's Sharia controversy and the persecution of non-Muslims was sown. Christians as a community in the North would continue to be seen as strangers, men and women who really did not belong. And by virtue of being strangers of course they were limited in what they could claim. From point of view of access to jobs, access to education, access to publicly owned media and land acquisition, Christians in the North would come to be seen as objects of pity. They were at the mercy of those who believed they own the land. From those earliest times, till now, Muslims have been accustomed to seeing themselves as superior to other citizens by virtue of living in an environment that treated them as first-class citizens and others as second-class citizens.

With political independence, non-Muslims in Northern Nigeria were told in no unclear terms that there were advantages in being Muslim. The first premier of Northern Nigeria, Alhaji Ahmadu Bello, the Sardauna of Sokoto, began a massive campaign for conversions to Islam across the North. Being a Muslim for example became the basis for ascending to any meaningful economic or political office in the region. The message was clear: if you wish to progress in the civil service, you have to convert to Islam; if you wish to thrive in business, you have to become a Muslim; if you wish to make progress as a politician, you need to convert to Islam.

At the level of traditional life, the non-Muslim population of Northern Nigeria have often been ruled by Muslim chiefs who often destroyed their social and traditional institutions. Those locals who wanted to rule over their people were largely required to convert to Islam since being a Muslim was considered a *conditio sine qua non* for ascension to the throne. This was in spite of the fact that those to be governed had their distinct culture and were not Muslims. This unjust situation persisted up till only recently, and it has been the basis of many conflicts and crisis situations in the Northern part of Nigeria.

The Sharia and the Crisis of Secularity in Nigeria

Since the birth of Nigeria's new political dispensation on May 29th, 1999, the *Sharia* more than anything else has threatened the stability of the state. How has this come about and what are the implications for the stability of the nation state? What are the implications for Christians and non-Muslims in Nigeria? It is important to note that by itself, the issue of the status of Islamic law has always been part of our national vocabulary. Way back in the late 1950s, just before independence, the Northern regional government had to send delegations to Sudan and Pakistan to make investigations about the status of Islamic law in plural societies. Their findings became the basis for the Penal Code which has been in existence. In the various Constitutional debates in Nigeria (1978/9, 1988/9 and 1995) the status of the Sharia law has proved to be problematic. However, in all these debates, the main issues have been how to address the issues of appeals arising from Lower Courts right to the Supreme Court. With only State Sharia Courts of Appeal in existence, the question centred around Muslims asking for what amounted to a Court of equal appellate status with the Supreme Court. But the argument of the experts has been that we cannot have two Supreme Courts in one country. This is how it was until after May 29th, 1999.

Since the declarations and then adoptions of Islamic Law as the legal system beginning with the State of Zamfara, most of the states of Northern Nigeria have adopted similar positions. Essentially, this problem, engineered by politicians was seen as part of the internal struggles to gain political space in Zamfara. As Governor Sanni Yerima succeeded and was turned into a hero, many other Governors came under pressure from their supporters to adopt the Sharia as the legal system. Christians in those states have been living with a persistent fear of harassment and intimidation. The Sharia law effectively turns the erstwhile secular state to an Islamic state, while the rights of non-Muslims are grossly limited or outrightly violated. Women are often the most affected by these changes in the legal status of the state. As it turns out, no one seems to be able to call the *Sharia* champions to order. So, where do we go from here? What are the implications for our national reconciliation, unity and peace?

Conclusion

In my opinion, the best weapon that can be used to contain the Sharia is, to a reasonable extent, the eradication of the acrimonious poverty, ignorance and massive unemployment that we witness in our land today. Those who have enlisted into the Sharia army, who have been used in the various riots across the North, are often from the motley crowd of uneducated and unemployed youth. In the Southern states where the Sharia is not an issue, this category of youths is also involved in one form of violence or the other. Either as Egbesu youths, or members of the OPC and Bakassi Vigilante groups, or a gang of armed robbers, these ignorant and unemployed youths have emerged to take the population hostage and unleash the reign of terror that the nation now witnesses with seeming helplessness.

The Sharia crisis must be located within the framework of the struggle for and the balance of power in Nigeria. We cannot discuss the secular status of the Nigerian state without a proper understanding of the issues that have made religion so important in the lives of so many people in Nigeria today. Inability to access power is a dangerous weapon when people are physically fit and ready to work but find themselves constrained. It is this ugly situation that selfish politicians are today exploiting with the introduction of the *Sharia*. True, the problems of poverty and illiteracy, brought about by the massive corruption of the ruling elite (Muslim and Christians) is what has led us to where we are today.

We shall get out of this impasse only through a massive investment in education and in projects that would provide gainful employment for the army of unemployed youths that are today roaming our streets. We shall get out of the mess only when we succeed in building a formidable civil society that will insist on the observance of the elementary principles of democracy and respect for the fundamental human rights of persons, including the right to freedom of conscience in a pluralistic society such as ours. We shall see the end to demonstrations, riots and killings over the Sharia when Nigerians become enlightened enough to vote into positions of leadership only those who are avowed to upholding each and every provision of the constitution of the Federal Republic of Nigeria. Yes, we shall know peace in Nigeria only when peace-loving Nigerians begin to take the elected representatives of the people to task with regard to their commitment or otherwise to creating the enabling environment for peace and social well-being. In the meantime, our national affairs seem to be in the hands of contract chasers, political bandits, callous opportunists and reckless dogs of power, and so no one is able to stop the madness of the Sharia. What can we do but give alms to Jangedi whose arm was cut in Zamfara for stealing a cow, and pray for the soul of Safiya, who may soon be executed in Sokoto for committing adultery alone!

CHAPTER ELEVEN

A Review of the Sharia Crisis in Nigeria
(Written on September 2, 2002)

Adoption of Sharia Law and the Attendant Tension and Conflicts

Amidst widespread protestation from non-Muslims and many level-headed Muslims in Nigeria, and at the consternation of the international community, the Sharia ill-wind has continued to blow through the Northern States of Nigeria like a devastating cyclone, consuming lives and creating tension in its wake. After the introduction of the controversial Islamic legal system in the North-western State of Zamfara on February 11, 2000, eleven other States of Northern Nigeria, including Katsina, Kano, Sokoto, Bauchi, Niger, Gombe, Jigawa, Bornu, Kebbi, Yobe and Kaduna States have followed suit. In each case, the Sharia controversy has been accompanied with tension. And in the case of Kaduna, which is populated perhaps equally by Christians and Muslims, the tension degenerated to very violent conflicts in February and May 2000, that saw to the death of thousands of Muslims and Christians, including a Catholic priest and a legislator.

The mere threat of the introduction of Sharia in predominantly Christian Plateau State led to the most brutal riots ever to take place in Jos during the second week of September 2001. The town with about the best weather conditions in Nigeria, popularly known as the land of peace and tourism, lost its innocence, as neighbours who had co-existed peacefully for decades, all of a sudden turned against each other, and sent hundreds to their early graves. Between February 2000 and March 2002, similar sharia-related riots have erupted in parts of Kaduna, Bauchi, Plateau, Niger and Nasarawa States. The tension generated by the Sharia all over the country has been such that a quarrel between two young people (one a Hausa Muslim and the other a Yoruba Christian) very quickly degenerated into an inter-ethnic and inter-religious conflict in which hundreds of lives were lost and millions of Naira worth of property were destroyed.

The implementation of the Sharia Law itself in the twelve Northern States where it now holds sway has been full of the tragic drama of not only brutal floggings in public for minor misdemeanours, but also it has robbed many poor victims of their hands or legs which were chopped off as punishment for petty stealing, and what is more, we may soon begin to witness in Nigeria death by stoning for women convicted of adultery, while their male partners are let off the hook for lack of evidence!

Individual Victims of Sharia Punishment

Malam Bello Jangedi was the very first victim of the repugnant Sharia punishment system in Nigeria. He was convicted for stealing a cow by a Sharia court in Zamfara State in the year 2000, and in spite of pleas for mercy from well-meaning people from within and outside Nigeria, he had his left arm amputated. Since then, many more people have fallen victim to this primitive legal system, losing not only hands and legs, but their fundamental rights and freedom as well. However, two cases have caught the attention of the world and provoked so much outrage from across the globe. They include the case of Safiya Husseini who in the year 2001 was condemned to death by stoning for adultery by a Sharia court in Sokoto State, while her partner was acquitted for lack of evidence. She was later discharged on technical grounds by a higher court. And now as we write this article there is the ongoing case of Amina Lawal whose death sentence by stoning (also for adultery), has been confirmed by the Katsina State Sharia Appeal Court, sending shock waves across the world and destroying whatever is left of the good name of Nigeria before the international community. Also, in the news these days is the case of two lovers (Ahmadu Ibrahim and Fatima Usman), found guilty of adultery by the Sharia court in Niger State, and sentenced to death by stoning.

On the whole the introduction of the Sharia to the Northern States has done the most damage so far to the Nigerian polity, after the (1967-1970) civil war against the secession bid of the Eastern Region. The delicate peace that existed between Muslims and Christians in the Northern part of Nigeria seems to have been destroyed. In place of peaceful co-existence, what we find in most of the North today is tension, a feeling of insecurity and occasional eruption of violence. Many

non-Muslims and non-indigenes of the affected states in the North, have
had to re-locate for fear that they might lose their lives during one of the
frequent conflicts or have their hands cut off for the flimsiest excuse, or
simply out of a realisation that their fundamental rights are no longer
guaranteed in these states.

Belated and Weak Reaction of Government

True, the Sharia crisis has been the greatest challenge that the post-
military era Nigeria has had to grapple with. But the Obasanjo
administration has not shown in any way that it can deal decisively with
the problem. Instead, the administration has watched as it were
helplessly as the evil of Sharia keeps threatening the stability of the
nation and its delicate democracy. Perhaps the only serious comment
made by the federal government since the Sharia saga started in February
2000 is the message sent to the Northern Governors a couple of months
ago by Kanu Agabi, the Justice Minister and Attorney General. In the
message which was sent in April 2002 (more than two years after the
Sharia became law in parts of the country), the Minister said:

> The fact that Sharia Law applies to only Muslims or to those who elect
> to be bound by it makes it imperative that the rights of such persons to
> equality with other citizens under the constitution be not infringed. A
> Muslim should not be subjected to a punishment more severe than
> would be imposed on other Nigerians for the same offence.

Warnings from the Catholic Bishops' Conference

However, soon after the Governor of Zamfara made public his intention
to impose Sharia law on the state early in the year 2000, the Catholic
Bishops Conference issued a stern warning to the Federal Government
and the people of Nigeria on the destructive potential of such an
unfortunate development, including a possible breakdown of law and
order, but the government did not heed the warning. In a memorandum
addressed to President Obasanjo on October 20, 1999, the Bishops
restated the secular status of the nation's constitution which forbids the
declaration of any religion as state religion in the country or any part of
it. They observed that the action of the Zamfara State Government is

not only unnecessary, but dangerous and harmful in the present context of Nigeria. The imposition of the Islamic Law on any part of the country "is putting an explosive device at the foundation of the unity and integrity of Nigeria," noting that "the country cannot survive as one organic entity if certain States decide to have laws of their own not only different from, but directly contrary to the laws of the land."

Yet the president took no action to halt the proposed imposition of the Sharia. It was launched in Zamfara State with much fanfare on February 22, 2000. The Bishops once again made a statement on the Sharia in a communique released after their plenary meeting of March 2000, and soon after the first Sharia riots in Kaduna where nearly 2000 lives were lost. They noted that "the issue of the Sharia and its place in the Constitution of the Federal Republic of Nigeria has continued to be a source of serious conflict." Then they declared that:

> We are committed to one Nigeria, where persons of different religious and ethnic traditions can live together in peace and harmony. We do not countenance the break-up of Nigeria, neither are we in favour of the split of Nigeria into different pockets, where one state lives under the constitution and a neighbouring state operates under another law.

At the end of their September 2000 meeting (which was held in the Northern State of Kaduna), the Bishops called on the government "to address the Sharia issue with the seriousness and sense of urgency that it deserves with a view to finding solutions that will bring the nation back to unity and harmony." They continued:

> Government, they said, "should desist from favouring one religion over others. Politicians too should refrain from using religion to further their political ambitions and sectional interests, knowing how this can easily divide the people and erupt into violence. The people, on their part, should be vigilant and refuse to be used as tools for the prosecution of the selfish agenda of unscrupulous politicians and other agents of destabilisation.

By this time many riots had taken place and many more thousands of lives had been lost and millions of Naira worth of property destroyed in the Sharia whirlwind, which was now spreading fast across the Northern States, yet President Obasanjo remained under the illusion that the entire project was the handiwork of a young rascally governor, which will not see the light of day. But now with twelve states of Northern Nigeria under the firm grip of the Islamic Law, and with many hands cut off and more women at risk of being condemned to death by stoning for adultery, Obasanjo and others who at the onset underestimated the danger are today confounded.

Brief Historical Background

How has this Sharia imbroglio come about and what are its implications for the future of the political entity we call Nigeria? What are the implications for Christians and other non-Muslims living in Nigeria? It is important to note that Islam was established in much of the territory known today as Northern Nigeria by means of the Jihad led by Uthman Dan Fodio in 1804. Sharia was practised to varying degrees in these areas until the British came on the scene about one hundred years after.

When the British took control of the territory, they discounted the application of Sharia in criminal cases because they considered many of the punishments primitive and repugnant. However, on the eve of Nigeria's independence in 1960, the "penal code" was devised to replace the criminal aspects of the Sharia for the North. Even though the code criminalised such things as adultery, it did not include the death penalty for any offence except murder, nor did it have such outrageous punishments as the cutting of hands and legs and the flogging of people in the public. But fundamentalist or fanatical Muslims in the North have always craved for the full implementation of the Sharia. The debate over the Sharia and its place in our secular constitution has come up now and again in Nigeria's evolving political history. It was however not too difficult to keep the tension down during the military dispensation, when the country was run in a unitary fashion, and when states had no legislative house of their own. With the emergence in May 1999 of civilian rule however the religious zealots who got into politics decided to ignore the constitution of the country and in their various states they launched a full-scale Sharia, declaring punishable (for example in Zamfara State), "any act declared to be an offence under the Quran, Sunnah and Ijtihad of the Maliki School of Islamic Thought."

The Catholic Church's Commitment to Religious Dialogue

The Catholic Church on its part remains very much committed to dialogue with other religions, including Islam. In one of their communiques referred to above (issued in March 2000), the Bishops called for dialogue as the way out of the current tension. They said, "we cannot but prefer dialogue to violence, and propose it as the way to collaboration, harmony, solidarity and unity." They called for the strengthening of all organs of inter-religious dialogue between Christians and Muslims in Nigeria. There is a powerful delegation of Catholics, including the President of the Bishops' Conference himself, in the Nigerian Inter-Religious Council, whose establishment the Government helped to facilitate.

The Bishops' Conference has also set up a Mission and Dialogue Department in the Catholic Secretariat to be engaged on an ongoing basis with Ecumenism and Inter-Religious Dialogue among other issues. The Secretary General of the Bishops' Conference attended the two Conferences hosted by Missio Aachen in Berlin in September 2001 and March 2002 and presented papers on the imperative of religious dialogue in Nigeria. And in June 2002, the Catholic Secretariat of Nigeria organised a Workshop on "Christian-Muslim Collaboration in the Building of Civil Society," at Abuja. It brought together members of the clergy, and lay representatives from all the Northern States with large Muslim population, as well as an Islamic Scholar and a delegate of Missio Aachen, to brainstorm on modalities for Christian-Muslim collaboration even in an environment charged with tension over the Sharia. Among the resolutions reached by the group are the following:

-   Dialogue between Christians and Muslims is very important because it will help clear the clouds of misunderstanding and create a better atmosphere of mutual enrichment.
-   Dialogue of action, communion and socio-political life should be promoted at all levels of society. These could include joint social projects, health facilities, economic ventures, etc, that will promote community development and peace.
-   Christian Women Organisations should reach out to counterpart Muslim organisations and work out common grounds for dialogue.
-   Christian and Muslim religious education should be such as will promote mutual respect and peaceful co-existence.

Conclusion

Christians and Muslims lay claim to equal proportion in the nation's 130 million population. So a secular state is the option for Nigeria. And while Christians will continue to reject the imposition of Sharia in any part of the country and insist on a secular constitution, the channels must always remain open for dialogue with the Muslim elite. The issue of the place of religion in the socio-political life of Nigeria can however not be adequately addressed if taken in isolation. The pitiable economic circumstances of many young, able-bodied people in the country and the real or perceived injustices in the socio-political and economic structures of the country do have a direct bearing on the ethnic and religious tension in the country today. Inability to access power by segments of the population is a dangerous thing. When people are physically fit and ready to work but find no work, their anger and frustration can sometimes find expression through fundamentalist religious activities.

We must concede that the problems of poverty and illiteracy, brought about by the massive corruption of the ruling elite (Muslim and Christians) has contributed a lot to where we find ourselves today. In the face of these odds, while Christian leaders and moderate elements within the Islamic elite, as well as human rights and pro-democracy advocates continue the struggle, we shall require the assistance of the international community in many ways. Beyond the need for partner agencies to assist with funding such programmes and projects that will help reduce poverty and ignorance and promote greater democratisation and conflict resolution towards peaceful co-existence, there is also the need for Western governments and agencies to constantly put pressure on the Nigerian leadership so that Nigeria may conform to international standards in the way the society is organised and run.

CHAPTER TWELVE

The Plight of Education and the Status of Teachers in Nigeria

(Paper presented at a Forum organized by the Federal Ministry of Education on "Cost and Financing of Education" in Nigeria, in Lagos, on September 17, 2002)

Too many things have happened within the last thirty years to the structure, the management, the administration, the supervision, and the financing of schools, colleges and universities in Nigeria, culminating in a serious dislocation of our educational system, whose symptoms are the much-decried fall in academic standards, widespread indiscipline, examination malpractice, frequent riots, and violent cult activities. Perhaps an even greater dislocation has occurred in the psyche of the contemporary Nigerian teacher, whose morale is now very low. The senseless politicisation of education at the Federal, State, and Local Government levels, the gross neglect of education in the allocation of funds by successive governments, and the shabby treatment of teachers of all cadres, have combined to rob education and the teaching profession of their traditional pride, dignity, and honour. It is as if a tragic war is being deliberately waged against the destiny of the people through the destruction of education, the very organ in which resides the hope of tomorrow.

The quality of life and work in our public schools and colleges, and the very environment in which teaching, and learning take place, have become a thing of shame and a source of embarrassment to many of us who have an idea of what educational institutions should look like. I consider myself fortunate for going through secondary school at the time I did. The economy of the country was buoyant, education was considered a viable venture worth investing in, and the population of the existing schools was manageable. Though there has always been corruption in this country, but by the time I went through primary and secondary schools, corruption in public life, and especially that aspect of corruption which involves the appropriation of public funds for private use had not assumed the monumental dimension of today. By then government schools were fairly adequately funded, and there was keen competition between government-owned schools and those owned by private agencies, especially the missions.

Soon after the civil war, most of the private schools were forcefully taken over by the state governments, and later this unjust appropriation was given legal backing with an obnoxious decree of the military government that was then in place. The teachers loved this development, because they automatically became civil servants and enjoyed all the privileges of that class. But the honeymoon lasted for only a while. As government monopolised the entire educational enterprise and took on both the regulatory and operational dimensions of education, the pack of cards soon came crashing down. And ever since then, the situation has gone from bad to worse. Almost all state-run schools and colleges are in a deplorable state. Most of the physical structures are in a state of total neglect and disrepair. The schools lack basic textbooks, laboratory equipment and other tools for imparting knowledge. Payment of salaries became epileptic. At a time when developments in educational technology have made computers, internet facilities, video recorders and overhead projectors necessary tools for adequate instruction in schools, our public schools often lack such elementary tools as the chalk or duster.

Some schools are unable to procure their class registers and record of work books several weeks into the term, while others often have to write their terminal or sessional examinations on the chalkboard, as there are no funds for the required stationery. The library shelves are often empty. Staff quarters, in schools where they used to exist, have now been abandoned by the staff to annual bush fire as the authorities have left them un-maintained and uncared-for for ages. Very few schools have staff buses, and even fewer staff members have vehicles, to the effect that many often have to trek miles to school on empty stomachs. Arriving in school tired and weary, they are often unable to perform. In most state-owned schools across the country, the teachers are faced with the onerous task of molding bricks without straws. This situation persists in spite of the recent improvement in the welfare of government workers.

Ladies and gentlemen, we have so destroyed the school system and the teaching profession, that the remnant of Nigerian teachers are largely a bunch of disgruntled, disillusioned, frustrated and depressed professionals. Lacking any motivation or encouragement, their output in terms of teaching, research and publication, is understandably low. The cumulative result of all these is not only that we are producing graduates of secondary schools, polytechnic, and universities, who cannot compete on equal terms with their counterparts trained elsewhere, but more painfully, that education is gradually losing its pride of place in the Nigerian society, and that the teaching profession has lost much of its status of honour and has rather become a despised and derided profession. I therefore salute all those who could explore other options but who have chosen to stay in Nigeria and remain in the teaching profession, for their resilience in the face of discouraging and demoralizing circumstances.

The project of education is supposed to be the promise of the future in any society, yet comparatively speaking, teachers are the least remunerated workers in the Nigerian economy. It is unusual today for a young graduate to wish to make a career out of teaching. Many pick up the chalk as a last resort, when all efforts to secure other jobs fail, and they remain in teaching only for as long as they are unable to find better jobs. Until very recently, practically every other job is better than teaching in Nigeria: That is why a PhD holder in History or Mathematics will rather queue up for a job with the Customs Department than take his chair at the University or College of Education. Yes, that is why a PhD holder in Economics will prefer the job of a counter cashier in a Commercial Bank, than that of a University teacher. Is it not true that a newly employed clerk in an oil company is often rated higher in our society than a primary school teacher with thirty years cognate experience?

Over the years the Nigerian teacher has become notorious for poverty, and so this noble career no longer attracts first class graduates from our universities. This situation cries out for immediate rectification, for when the institutions set up for the pursuit of knowledge are despised and those who transmit this knowledge from one generation to the other are in disrepute, then the future is in jeopardy. If the progressive collapse in the educational sector is allowed to continue, no one shall be spared; not even the children of the rich who are sent overseas, for they would come back to reap the harvest of decay in the Nigerian educational sector.

We must say that the crisis in the Nigerian educational set-up is an index of the country's socio-political equilibrium. Yes, the rupture in our institutions of learning is a measure of the communal health of this country. Indeed, the rapid deterioration of our public schools is an indictment on the successive leaders of our nation, for their failure to design and execute a viable policy on education or their outright prodigality with the project of education in this country. Nigeria does not lack the human and material resources necessary to redeem our educational enterprise. Nigeria does not lack the technical know-how to turn things around for the better. Nigerians have the means to establish and run schools that are schools, not breeding grounds for thieves, thugs and touts. What we lack is the political will to make things happen. We must summon this will and act now, if we are not to kill tomorrow before today's sun sets.

We call for an urgent re-orientation of the Nigerian citizenry on the place of education in the collective destiny of a people. We call for de-politicization in the establishment and administration of schools, and in the hiring and firing of teachers. We call for a re-prioritization in the allocation and management of our human and material resources, giving education the pride of place it deserves. We call for a re-formulation of our educational goals, principles, and policies, with the aim of demolishing sterile and superfluous structures, of decentralizing the management set-up, and of reducing to the barest minimum the usual bureaucracies of government as far as education is concerned.

CHAPTER THIRTEEN

Help! Maniacs Are in Power
(Written on November 11, 2002)

History is full of examples of leaders who grew into full-blown demoniacs, exhibiting manic traits that brought pain, misery and death to countless of their people. From Europe's Adolf Hitler of mid twentieth century, whose outsized megalomania brought about the extermination of six million Jews and numerous others, to Africa's Mobutu Sese Seko of the former Zaire who, at the height of his megalomania was allegedly richer than his country. Megalomania is a mental disorder that is characterised by delusion of power, wealth and grandeur. The megalomaniac has an uncontrollable impulse to acquire more and more power and appear bigger and bigger in the eyes of people, even if in the process he has to kill people who may be in his way.

Kleptomania on the other hand is a mental disorder of manic proportion which triggers in the sufferer a compulsive urge to grab and grab everything he finds, even if he has to steal the very lifeblood of others. The kleptomaniac must steal, even when the object of theft is not of any use to him. It is true that corruption has long been identified as a cancer in our society. But if our latter-day experiences are anything to go by, kleptomania will adequately define the manic condition that has afflicted Nigeria's successive torturers who in self-delusion have called themselves leaders.

Over the years the Nigerian ruling class (both military and their civilian successors), have sought to acquire through the looting and pillaging of the national treasury, the wealth they need to make them the richest in the land, hoping thereby to gain legitimacy and identity. Then by self-perpetuation, self-succession and self-regeneration they recycle themselves as the champions of Nigeria's politics and governance. But from the recent accusations and counteraccusations by distinguished senators and honourable men and women of the house of assembly, about huge financial inducements that are the order of the day in the National Assembly, "kleptocracy" rather than "democracy" seems to be the fitting cognomen for our own brand of government. Having been delivered from military autocracy by divine providence, Nigeria still has to contend with pathological thieves, rogues and scavengers whose uncontrollable impulse to accumulate wealth rides in tandem with their outsized ambition to remain in power.

Where in a couple of years many of our lawmakers who went in as paupers, have become multi-millionaires due largely to the thieving culture that we call settlement, I am convinced that the mania in our society has reached an alarming proportion. Where illegal access to state wealth has become so brazen that stacks of Naira notes meant for bribery are sometimes competing for space with the mace at the National Assembly, I am convinced that the demoniac has indeed been let loose. Call it whatever we wish, the current system is surviving on monumental pillars of corruption. Corruption is a pandemic national perversion that the civil society must address squarely, as another round of elections are around the corner.

A few years ago, someone did a reflection in which he delineated four broad levels of corruption in Nigeria as follows: *petty corruption* - practised by public servants who may be basically decent individuals but who are grossly underpaid, and who depend on small bribes from the public to feed their families and educate their children; *episodal corruption* - where honest behaviour is the norm, and corruption is the exception, and where dishonest public servants are disciplined when detected; *systemic corruption* - where the socio-economic and political system depends on corruption for its own survival; and *grand corruption* - where higher public officials and politicians make policies and regulations, or decide on the award of large contracts and projects which are motivated not by the need of the people, but by the greed of the legislator or the awarding official. What we seem to be witnessing among the governing elite in Nigeria belongs more to the last category of grand corruption. And this is happening in a regime that started out with a clear commitment to fight the evil of corruption.

This national cancer must be fought and destroyed. But total cure for this sick nation must involve multifarious attacks on many fronts. It will involve a review of the benefits of public office in Nigeria which appear to be too tempting for even the most "born again" Christian or the most acclaimed Islamic zealot that finds his or her way into politics in Nigeria. We need a re-conception of governance and a restructuring of government in Nigeria. We need to develop in potential office holders a keen sense of the common good. We need to device new ways of instilling in the leadership of this nation the virtues of accountability, answerability, and responsibility. For as presently constituted and maintained, government at all levels is too self-serving, too costly, and too prone to corruption.

We must entrench into the statute books, provisions for the recovery of stolen loot from offenders and their proximate beneficiaries, without time limit. Thereafter the nation must be on the watch and make it impossible for thieves and rogues to seize the nation's sovereignty. And going by our antecedents, is it out of place to request all who genuinely wish to lead the Nigerian people in the future to visit both the exorcist and the psychiatrist, just to ascertain their sanity and their freedom from the destructive demon of greed or the pathological state of kleptomania?

For those who believe in divine justice and have faith in the supremacy of the Creator, prayers do work miracles to deliver the supplicant. Recourse to prayer can become a potent instrument in our search for a cure to the nation's complex ailment. Anyone in doubt only needs to reflect upon our experience in June 1998. Prayers are recommended for leaders wishing to serve in the next dispensation. They need prayers to acquire divine wisdom and guidance in giving service to the people while escaping the mania from which the nation now lies prostrate. Our leaders need to pray to enter the nation's roll of honour after leaving office, and not to be remembered long after their time for being agents of national shame and infamy.

On my own part, I pray that the Almighty God may save our nation from corrupt chieftains, reckless looters and callous scavengers, who now camouflage as leaders of the people, along with their agents and allies at all levels. These self-proclaimed leaders of the people have for the umpteenth time plundered the commonwealth and infected the entire environment with the demon of greed and avarice. But as the election year 2003 approaches, I pray that the good Lord may save us from the hands of these punitive overlords.

As I pray for the poor, traumatised masses of Nigeria, I also pray for those who have inflicted so much misery and pain on them. I know that no one who steals or appropriates for himself or herself alone what belongs to all, can escape the supreme justice of God. I also know that no one who gives or takes bribe, and in that way compromises justice and fair play, can escape the inevitable retribution of our God. I therefore pray that the thieves, the rogues, the looters, the mercenaries and the scavengers in our midst, whose nefarious activities have put our nation in a state of perpetual distress, will repent today of their sin, before the Lord makes his next providential visit to Nigeria. For I know that when he comes, he shall flush out these cancerous outgrowths from our national landscape, so that uprightness may rise and flower once again in the land. I know that when he comes, he shall disinfect the land with his holy breath and discharge those evil parasites to *gehena!*

CHAPTER FOURTEEN

Addressing the Menace of Religious Fanatics in Nigeria
(Written on November 24, 2002)

Amid widespread protestation from non-Muslims and many level-headed Muslims in Nigeria, and at the consternation of the international community, an Islamic fundamentalist ill-wind has continued to blow through the Northern States of Nigeria like a devastating cyclone, consuming lives and property and aggravating the state of distress in the land. The latest mayhem is a fall-out of the botched Miss World competition in Nigeria. It happened like this: A journalist observed the scores of beauty queens from all over the world, and unwittingly wrote (in the Saturday November 17, 2002, edition of *This Day*, Newspaper), that the girls are so beautiful, that "even Muhammed would not have been able to resist some of them."

Apparently for Islamic fundamentalists, this is a blasphemous statement for which the author and everyone and everything related to him or her must be hounded to death or razed down. So, on Monday November 19, the Islamic zealots made for the office of the Newspaper in Kaduna and razed it down along with any vehicles carrying its name. But their anger was not assuaged. Supposing the Newspaper to be owned by a Southern Christian, they made for any Christian or Southern person or property in site, killing, maiming and burning. Over one hundred lives have been lost so far, and the dust is yet to settle. We have been reliably informed that all the Churches and other structures belonging to Christians in Tudun Wada, and Kabala have been destroyed. Mission houses and presbyteries were also attacked and destroyed. Among those lying critically ill in the hospital today is an elderly priest, Father Iyere, who retired about ten years ago as Director of the Catholic Chaplaincy Services in the Nigerian Armed Forces.

Notable among the most valuable Catholic properties destroyed in this mayhem is the Catholic Resource Centre - a social development resource facility for the northern provinces of the Catholic Church. Rev.

Father Peter Tanko, Director of the Centre, who also resides there, narrowly escaped death by scaling the wall of his fence and fleeing to the neighbouring compound where he watched the looting and eventual burning of his house, office and vehicles. Thus, once again Kaduna has been brought to a standstill by Islamic fundamentalists. But that is not all. Abuja has had a taste of the deadly poison of Islamic fundamentalism, meaning that even the capital city of Nigeria which we thought was a melting pot, is not seen by the Muslims to belong to all Nigerians equally. After their Jumat prayers in Abuja on Friday November 22nd, and without any warning, thousands of irate youths, coming out of the mosque, chanted their usual war songs (*Alahu Akbar*), and descended on innocent motorists and passers-by, causing pandemonium in the city.

Many people who could not respond to questions posed to them in Arabic received machete cuts, while a number of cars belonging to non-Muslims were burnt or destroyed. The number of deaths arising from the Abuja uprising has not been ascertained as at the time of writing. The irate Islamic youths of Abuja were said to be venting their anger over the hosting of the Miss World Competition in Nigeria, and the unholy comment in the *This Day Newspaper* against the person of prophet Muhammed. Meanwhile, the Newspaper which has a number of Muslims at every level in its employment has on daily basis since Monday November 18th been publishing an apology to all Muslims for the "offensive" publication. But for the zealots, the apology is too little, and too late. For them, the harm has been done, and must be avenged, ostensibly on all non-Muslim Nigerians and their properties!

Now with a dusk to dawn curfew in Kaduna, and with thousands of heavily armed security agents taking over the streets of Abuja, there is uneasy calm in both cities. No one can say when normalcy will return, especially to Kaduna, as Christian youths, who were taken unawares this time around, may still be poised for a revenge mission. And for residents of Abuja, what happened last Friday is an indication that Abuja may not be the home of peace and security that the founders thought it would be for Nigerians of all creeds and ethnic nationalities.

Since February 2000, Sharia-related violent riots during which hundreds of lives are lost, and churches, shops, cars and houses belonging to Christians are burnt, have become a regular feature in Kaduna, Kano, Jos, Zaria and Bauchi, where a large population of

Christians live alongside Muslims. Innocent Christians and Southerners carrying on their legitimate businesses in the Northern States have either had to relocate down South or have lived in perpetual fear of the murderous gang of Islamic fanatics whose thirst for the blood of non-Muslims in their midst is now shown to be insatiable.

Kaduna has by all standards become the most dangerous place to live in Nigeria. After the Sharia-induced massacres of February and May 2000, the metropolitan city has been effectively divided into two, the River Kaduna marking the dividing line. Christians moved away from the Muslim-dominated northern flank of Tudun Wada, Unguwar Sarki, Unguwar Sanusi, Rigasa, Mando, Kabala and Kawo, and joined their fellows in the southern flank of Barnawa, Narayi, Sabo, Kakuri, where they now constitute the overwhelming majority, forcing some of the Muslims in the area to move away from there. In fact, some indigenes of Kaduna are actually asking that two different towns be created from the old Kaduna, one for Muslims, with a Muslim (Sharia) government, if the inhabitants so wish, and the other part for Christians, under the constitution of the Federal Republic of Nigeria. And since a large proportion of the entire state, south of the city of Kaduna is Christian, many are actually asking for a Southern Kaduna State to be created out of the present one.

What we have been witnessing in Nigeria in the last few years, is actually the failure of state and the collapse of governance. There is nothing on the ground to demonstrate that ours is not a land run over by political bandits, ethnic warlords and religious fanatics. The average citizen now seems to have lost confidence in the capacity of those in power to protect lives and property. Where one part of the country can decide to operate an Islamic legal code that is clearly at variance with the national constitution, cutting off the limbs of petty offenders, condemning poor adulterers to death by stoning, and harassing non-Muslims every so often, the impression created is that no one is in charge of our affairs, and there is no law and order in place.

With a selfless, visionary and prudent leadership, the thousands of deaths we have recorded, and the millions of Naira worth of property that have been destroyed in the last few years, could have been avoided. We hold the current leadership of the Nigerian State responsible for the massive destruction of lives and property in Kaduna, Jos, Kano, Zaria, Bauchi and elsewhere over the Sharia controversy, and at the hands of

Islamic fundamentalists, because the president and his team have remained indolent and insensitive in the face of a very explosive situation. We hold President Obasanjo and his team accountable for the blood and tears in many parts of Nigeria where non-Muslims have lost their right to live in peace, for it is the primary duty of government to protect innocent and law-abiding citizens from the nefarious activities of hooligans, bandits and fanatics. We hold them responsible for the pain and anguish that is the lot of the innocent citizens of Northern Nigeria who have been rendered refugees in their own country, because we expect them to own up to their ineptitude and resign from their high office, if their being in office makes no difference for the internal security of the nation.

After three and a half years in government, the present crop of leaders have done little to improve the lot of Nigerians. The economy is comatose. Unemployment, especially graduate unemployment has soared, as a result of which the mass of our young people are losing hope. Our schools, hospitals, and other social infrastructure are in an embarrassing state of decay. The population itself is more divided today than it was since the end of 1967-1970 civil war. And now religious violence has been added to our multiple woes. But in the midst of all these calamities, our leaders carry on business as usual. They are feeding fat on our scarce resources, selling the poor for a pair of sandals and playing games with the fate and fortune of our children. There are allegations and counter-allegations of bribery, running into hundreds of millions of Naira, and involving high-ranking members of the legislature and the executive. Young Nigerians have become angry, restive and violence-prone. They are capitalising on anything they can find to vent their anger. Yesterday it was ethnicity. Today it is religion. Tomorrow it may be political affiliation. And there are politicians who fan these flames of violence for their own selfish political advantage. But where does all this leave Nigeria?

In the midst of the madness of today peace-seeking Nigerians must begin to take the elected representatives of the people to task with regard to their commitment or otherwise to creating the enabling environment for peace and social well-being. The saner elements in our society must begin to take the president, the governors, the local government chairmen and the lawmakers at all levels to task on their capacity or otherwise to formulate and defend such legal instruments and pursue such policies that will make for peace, security and prosperity.

It is not enough for us to desire peace for our land. We must be peacemakers as well. We must be committed to designing strategies to forestall, manage and resolve conflict situations. We must work hard and make sacrifices towards the attainment of the peace of our dream. The men and women of goodwill in Nigeria must constantly be on the watch to ensure that in our evolving democracy, such agents of destabilisation as the gang of Islamic fanatics in the North and their collaborators elsewhere do not hijack our commonweal for selfish political gains, and transform our land to a theatre of war, a war with no discernible reason and one without frontiers.

The latest uprising in Kaduna and Abuja should teach despondent Nigerians that evil will always thrive when good people keep silent. Christians and the saner segment of the Islamic community must reflect together and rise up in defence of the secular nature of our national constitution, or else Nigeria may soon become another Algeria. A stitch in time saves nine, they say. This latest event in the tragic drama of the Nigerian state is one more reason why it is necessary to hold a roundtable or a national conference to discuss the terms of our social contract as a nation. We cannot continue to be banded together in a hellish state by professional politicians who are only mercenaries, as they have little or no concern for the flesh and blood of the poor that are sacrificed on daily basis to an insatiable god of hate. The time to act is now!

CHAPTER FIFTEEN

The Problem with Nigeria
(Written on November 24, 2002)

As a people we Nigerians have a penchant for making scapegoats of fellow citizens whom we perceive as the cause of our many woes. We see such individuals or groups as the "enfants terribles" of our national calamities, and so we demonise them, while maintaining a self-righteous disposition ourselves and absolving our own group (ethnic, religious or political) of any blame. Yet, in truth, we know that it is a cross-section of Nigerians from North and South and from East and West that have ruined our nation so badly and wrecked its economy so callously. We know that those whose evil behaviour brought a curse upon our land include the Igbo and the Hausa, the Yoruba and the Tiv, the Urhobo and the Efik, the Fulani and the Bini.

We know in truth that it is a collection of Nigerians of all creeds that have conspired to loot this nation and stack the proceeds of their looting in foreign vaults, while abandoning the generality of the people to poverty and misery. In truth we know that it is Nigerians of all political persuasions that have over the years presided over the gang-rape which has left our nation in the present state of pain and shame. Yet we find it very convenient to point our fingers at that other person, and those other groups (apart from ourselves and our group) that must be held responsible for our national predicament.

We Nigerians are also notorious for our tendency to give single and simplistic explanations to complex national issues, in this way dodging the challenges and sacrifices that must be made by all in the difficult process of nation-building. We find it convenient for example to blame military rule alone for our multifarious national problems. We find it convenient to ascribe our delicate social equation to an all-embracing domination of one group or section of the country over others. We find it convenient to blame the ground-shaking social upheaval we experience today on either ethnicity or religion, whereas many of our inter-ethnic or inter-religious skirmishes have roots that are deeper and more deadly, roots that are moral and spiritual and not just political or economic.

Events on the ground have consistently demonstrated that the alleged North-South or East-West divide is often exaggerated, for Nigerians of diverse ethnic and religious backgrounds have an incredible capacity to quarrel and quickly settle afterwards, living together and even sharing household utensils. Particularly at the lower level of society, Nigerians have consistently demonstrated that social barriers are oftentimes artificial, opaque, crisis-induced and non-permanent. They have often demonstrated that living together can be as peaceful, mutual and natural as God designed it to be.

Our fundamental problem as a nation therefore is not the North-South divide, although it must be admitted that there are divisive elements in the structural arrangements between the North and the South. Our fundamental problem is not exactly about who controls what resources either, although the oil producing regions such as the Niger Delta have suffered extensive deprivation which calls for substantial redress. And despite the violence occasioned by the threat of the Sharia law in some states in Northern Nigeria, and the very tense debate over its place in our nation's constitution, religion nevertheless does not constitute the fundamental problem of the Nigerian state, for politics aside, Nigerians have over the years demonstrated an incredible capacity to live together with their various creeds. The above problems, serious as they sometimes appear, are often incidental, not fundamental. These problems are often symptomatic of the failure of a state whose leaders lack vision, charism, integrity and commitment, and whose people stink with corruption and indiscipline.

The real problem fundamental to the retarded progress of this country resides in the primordial greed and avarice, the crass materialism and selfishness, the wickedness and callousness that are to be found among the various groups that populate the land. The more fundamental problem with Nigeria is to be found in the privatisation of the state by individual members of the elite class, who have often cashed in on, and exploited the long-standing ethnic antipathies in the land. The more fundamental problem with Nigeria is the callous neglect of the common good by the leaders as they pursue the politics and economics of greed.

The challenge before Nigerians today is how to transform the citizenry from the less human state of ignorance, social injustice, violence and death to the more human state of heightened awareness, justice, fairness, peace and prosperity. The challenge before us is how to transit from the less human state of hatred, resentment, selfishness, greed, corruption and indiscipline to the more human state of love, mutual forgiveness, solidarity, concern for the common good, and the fear of God.

The challenge before Nigerians is first to acknowledge the past sins and atrocities, we have dealt on one another either as individuals or in our social groups, and then in truth to be ready to show contrition. We need to acknowledge the mistakes, deficiencies and weaknesses in the structures around which our society is configured, and we must be prepared to boldly make amends. We must acknowledge that our unspoken prejudices, our pet hates and our uncharitable demonstration of intolerance, have intermittently exploded in inter-ethnic and religious strife and imploded in intra-tribal violence. We must acknowledge that the wounds and hurts in our historical and social development remain festering, and we must acknowledge the need to offer and receive forgiveness. If ever a real forum for national dialogue is convened for Nigerians, by whatever name it is called, this will be a number one task for such a forum.

A major challenge before us is how to change our conception of leadership. We must begin to see leadership as stewardship and not as an opportunity to exploit the people in every way for personal aggrandizement. It is time for us to re-examine our structures and undertake essential and far-reaching reformation to change the country's leadership profile for the better. And when a forum for national dialogue is convened, this will constitute one more item in the agenda.

Nigerians need to know that the good leader should be ready to make sacrifices for the common good. Those who aspire to leadership positions must have a sense of mission and vision. They must have a passion for the poor, the weak and those on the margins of society. Nigerians must be clear about what the good leader is not. The good leader is not the idle Nigerian politician who is in politics for the spoils of office, one whose only visible profession is politics and who has no other viable means of sustainable support. The good leader is not the feudalist ruler whose historical foundations, structured as they often are on ignorance, are antithetical to democratic principles. Feudalist authority structures are still very much around us, in the form of traditional rulers. They wield considerable influence over a gullible population. Yet they are part of the nation's fundamental problems. They often think nothing of holding down the subjects in penury and serfdom, while feeding fat on the blood and tears of the very flock they are supposed to shepherd. Examples abound in our recent history to show how traditional rulers from North to South, and from East to West are among the foremost enemies of the Nigerian people.

Finally, the challenge before Nigerians is how to develop a new sense of national cohesion, a new sense of patriotism, and a new vision of Nigeria as our true homeland. We must get to work and develop for ourselves a new civilisation that will turn hate into love, a new civilisation that will transform foes into friends and a new civilisation that will change pretentious leaders into true stewards of the people. For unless and until we come by this new vision and civilisation, by which greed, avarice, corruption, hatred, primitive feudalism and the manipulation and exploitation of religion and ethnicity are destroyed, the Nigerian nation will yet remain distressed and its people traumatised. Unless and until this moral transformation takes place in the hearts of individuals and groups, not even a sovereign national conference will save our land.

CHAPTER SIXTEEN

Nigerian Democracy and the Politics of Absurdity
(Paper delivered to "Christian Women in Politics,"
in Lagos, December 8, 2002)

Introduction

I congratulate Roli Adeniyi and her friends who have conceived the very noble idea of Christian Women in Politics. I call it a very noble idea, because for forty-two years, men have held this country hostage, and I agree that it is time the women took over. I believe that they cannot do worse than the men have done. Chances are that they would do better. In our society, and indeed in every society, Christian women have an enormous responsibility, as mothers, nurturers, administrators, and builders of the home, endowed by nature with rare beauty, intuition, love, generosity, self-sacrifice, and compassion, to champion the cause of restoring the nation back to the path of integrity, when the men, consumed as usual by greed and aggression have ruined the country and devastated the landscape. So, for me, today's event is a welcome development in our nation's political evolution.

Karl Maier, a renowned journalist, published a book on Nigeria in the year 2000 in which he critically reviewed the many failures and contradictions that make peace and prosperity a tall dream for our country. He gave the book the curious title: *"This House Has Fallen"* (Penguin Books, 2000). I read through the book with a sense of shame and embarrassment, for in the event of this house really falling apart, I do not carry another country's passport. I have no other place to call home, yet I cannot fail to agree with him that as presently configured and with the conduct of our male-dominated leadership class, this political entity is only a pack of cards.

It was Charles de Gaulle who said that politics is too serious a business to be left for politicians alone. The project of the structuring of society, the distribution of resources, the maintenance of law and order, the protection of lives and property, the provision of social, economic, agricultural, industrial and health infrastructures, and the protection of the citizens of a country from external attack, which make up what we call governance, cannot, and must not, be left entirely in the hands of the men whom we call professional politicians in Nigeria. Many of these professional politicians have often demonstrated over the years that they are not genuine democrats or true patriots, but neo-feudalists, contract chasers, callous mercenaries, and prostitutes of power who are out only to steal, to cheat, and to destroy. We cannot leave our fate and fortune in the hands of these machismo, who have no milk of human kindness, who have no compassion for the poor and the weak, and who, when voted into power become aggressors and dominators rather than protectors and nurturers of the people. That is why all hands must be on deck and all serious-minded groups and individuals of talent and vision (including the Christian Women in Politics), must be passionately engaged in the project of national reconstruction which in my view demands first of all an ethical revolution or a process of moral regeneration.

Nigeria's Flirtation with Absurdity

Nigeria has had a long romance with values and practices that are antithetical to democracy. Though there is no perfect model of democracy to be found anywhere in the world, our own variant of democracy bears the marks of deliberate manipulations and imperfections. Democracy is on trial in Nigeria, not just on account of our leaders who constantly seek to domesticate the globally recognised principles of this modern system of governance for private political and economic advantage, but also on account of the generality of the people who are largely ignorant, apathetic, and despondent, and who do not seem to be in a hurry to escape from the hangover of military rule. In the collision and confusion of our individual and group perceptions of governance, the true meaning of democracy is lost, and that is why peace and progress remain in flight from our country.

The game of politics in today's Nigeria can be rightly described as a free-for-all. After the nightmare of military rule, Nigerian politicians are once again showing political delinquency. They are once again approaching politics with an incredible measure of indiscipline and reckless abandon as of yore. They have forgotten so soon the political bondage we were all in and the imperative for us to reject the resurrection of politics with bitterness. We must not run away from the truth: acrimonious politics has been the bane of Nigerian politics from way back in our history. This ugly situation is played out everywhere right across the country as people jostle for political space. But political acrimony may be assuming unprecedented dimensions and intensity now more than ever before, and sadly, this political canvas is leaving in its wake more blood and tears for a people that have been stretched to breaking point by illiteracy, poverty, and widespread unemployment.

It is said that the chain of society is as good as its weakest link. But the way we have been operating and interpreting our new-found democracy in Nigeria leaves much to be desired. We have been pursuing the business of governance with a killer's touch, using all manner of unsavoury maneuvres to gore at political adversaries. And as the year 2003 elections draw near, our largely male-dominated political class appears set inexorably on a deadly trail. Just take a look at the conduct of the National Assembly members among themselves, and their relationship with the Presidency. See the endless war in Enugu and Anambra States. How do you place the acrimony and rancour that we witness within each political party and between the parties?

True, Nigerians are back in the business of the politics of confusion, and one would query the underlying motives of many a Nigerian politician. For some, the game is *politics of convenience.* For some more it is *politics of the belly.* For many more, it is *politics for survival,* and a *do-or-die affair.* This is to say that people are in it for want of anything else meaningful to do for sustenance, and they would kill and maim to retain their meal ticket. In this deadly enterprise, survival strategies often attract the rules of unfair competition. We must recognise in the atmosphere of political confusion currently holding sway in the land, the seeds of discord in our polity and remove them with dispatch. If we fail to do so, we run the risk of harvesting political conflicts by the bushel, come year 2003, and women are among those who would suffer most when the worst happens.

Nigerian politicians appear ill-equipped and unprepared to outgrow political immaturity. Why are we not disposed to respect constitutional processes for democratic political change? Why are our politicians so intent on fighting to the death and foisting their selfish political agenda on the people? If not propelled by greed and greed alone, why are our politicians so bitterly locked in inter-party and intra-party disagreement and bitterness? Why are they so deeply immersed in the politics of personalities and not issues, if not to assuage their greed and count the political returns? It must be remembered that genuine hunger can be managed in many ways, but there is no way of managing greed, for while the world can sustain the needs of millions of its people, it cannot slake the thirst of one greedy person in power.

The True Meaning of Democracy

Democracy is and means much more than the holding of elections. The classical definition of democracy is that of Abraham Lincoln in his Gettysburg address of 1863. He said inter alia that democracy is the "government of the people by the people and for the people." Democracy is not an open license to executive lawlessness or legislative recklessness. Democracy is not a free ticket for deadly political brinkmanship. Democracy is not a game of conquest. It is not the crushing of opposing views or the scalping of opponents. It is not the ascendancy of greed and the unrestrained gathering of the spoils of war by a few smart thugs. Instead, democracy is a game of compromise. It is the meeting point of disparate opinions. It is about respect for the rights and opinions of others. Democracy is about free association and the making of free choices in an environment devoid of fear and intimidation. It is about the establishment of societal order, the protection of civil rights and the acceptance of civic responsibility. It is about the promotion of the common good or the welfare of everyone in the society.

Democracy is the rule of law. It is about the equality of all persons under the law. It is about keeping faith with a people's constitution, giving voice to the minority, and providing for the weakest members of the society. Democracy is about the sanctity of the institutions that superintend the social contract between the leaders and the rest of society. It is about submission to the independent judicial arbitration of the courts. It is about the upholding of high ethical standards for aspirants to public office. The democratic culture is characterised by checks and balances. It involves the process of feedback and recall, which together guarantee accountability. It is averse to dictatorship, autocracy, and authoritarianism. Democracy negates self-perpetuation in power against the self-expression of the people It is averse to the transformation of leaders into absolute monarchs. A situation whereby elected representatives habitually foist their "wisdom" on the people is antithetical to democracy. Leaders in a democratic setting understand that the power of the opinion of the people is a price they must bear for democratic leadership. Why, for example, would our present leaders reject the strident call for some form of national forum or conference to deal with grave and fundamental issues of our corporate existence? When will our leaders concede that there are times when national dialogue or referendum becomes imperative?

Observers of our politics are discomfited by the quality of our political discourse and the sources and causes of our political cleavages. Modern democratic political practice is about informed debate, differences of opinion and approach and the forging of compromise on issues of governance. But here, we are consumed by mutual hatred induced by the perceived loss of political opportunities and the inordinate impatience to await our turn next time around. There is demonstrable lack of ideological content in our political disagreements.

We are hardly ever engaged in the conflict of ideas on substantive issues of development. For if the welfare of the people were the cause of the conflicts on the ground, it would be understood. If differences in opinion regarding the provision of qualitative education, employment generation, social and health infrastructure were the cause of the conflicts, it would have been understood. Yes, indeed, if these kinds of issues were the principal raison d'etre for our political cleavages, carpet-crossings and conflicts, our politics would not have been laced with so much rancour. But we all know that the ulterior motive behind much of our political acrimony is how to align behind power bases and how to access resources in the service of self. But the generality of Nigerians must begin to discriminate between the desire for genuine political service on the one hand and insatiable greed, political ambition, and opportunism on the other.

The Challenge before Political Aspirants and Citizens

There are numerous challenges ahead for all who desire leadership positions in the coming dispensation, and women aspirants should particularly take note of them: Our national economy is in pretty bad shape. Economic development goes begging in a land harbouring natural and human resources of tremendous value. The few non-oil sector industries we have are operating by far below installed capacity. The internal security of this country is in a precarious state. Our urban streets are teeming with hundreds of thousands of youths and children hawking, extorting, begging, or simply loitering all day. Many unemployed youths have taken to armed robbery, hooliganism, and banditry. Others have become totally disoriented, and in need of rehabilitation. Our elderly who toiled so hard to bring up the younger generation of Nigerians lack social security in their old age and are pleading for attention. On the whole, the masses who eke out a living in a land as naturally blessed as ours and who are the pawns in the hands of politicians, need attending to.

As another round of elections approaches, this is the time for Nigerians to ask the questions: Who are the aspirants to political office this time around? What are their antecedents? What kind of people were they in private life or public office? How have they performed in the various positions of responsibility they have held in the past? What kind of husbands have they been to their wives? What kind of fathers have they been to their children? What measure of patriotism and sense of service have they demonstrated in their previous outings? What is their understanding of the common good? How do they hope to meet the challenge of national reconciliation and economic rejuvenation?

After suffering for so long at the hands of callous scavengers who camouflaged as politicians in our land, Nigerians should start recognising the immense power in their votes and resolutely reject those neo-feudalists in our midst who have no qualms of conscience living in affluence and conspicuous consumption, while the rest of the people whom they claim to represent wallow in acrimonious poverty. After years of national desolation at the hands of mercenaries who claimed to be leaders, Nigerians should start learning to reject with their voting power those nonentities who in the past preyed on the gullibility of the ignorant poor and the apathy and despondency of the educated few. True, the mass of Nigerians must make the connection between their destitution today and the debauchery of their successive rulers and show some measure of discernment regarding those who offer themselves for political office. We must all together brace up for action, and not only guard our freedom jealously, but also watch those who offer to serve in government carefully, constantly dragging their feet as close as possible to the fire of democracy.

I challenge the level-headed women in this country to summon the courage to be torch bearers of a new Nigeria, when we finally put to rest the lost generation of neo-feudalists, ethnic warlords, chronic kleptomaniacs, and callous plunderers. I challenge the Christian Women in Politics and others who are full of goodwill to rise up with determination and tell the macho men who have always been at the helm of affairs in our land, and who have made so much mess of it, that the greatest threat to human fulfilment and societal prosperity is not some external enemy, but (as St. Augustine puts it) "the want of order in the soul."

Conclusion

Organisations like Christian Women in Politics should take up the challenge of being torch bearers of a new Nigeria. As champions of truth, they must tell the men and women of our country that truth and justice are the pathways to peace, security and social well-being, and so every time truth is violated, the seed of violence and disorder is sown. Let all those who along with these Christian Women are disenchanted with the present circumstances and who are praying for the emergence of a new Nigeria constantly drum it to the ears of our countrymen and women that lies, falsehood and half-truths have never and will never nurture a people. Let the faithful remnant of Nigeria who are repulsed by the current triumph of mediocrity speak the truth loudly and forcefully that whenever lawlessness becomes the norm and illegality becomes the rule in any society, the superstructure soon comes crashing down. Yes, let the torch bearers of a new Nigeria, who hold the hope of a new dawn, rise up with determination, and demonstrate, not only with their lips, but also with the conduct of their public and private lives, that corruption is a cancer that eats its own host to death, but that righteousness exalts a nation.

CHAPTER SEVENTEEN

Nigeria Police and Our Moral Degeneracy
(Written on August 12, 2003)

In recent times the Police in Nigeria and the manner of their operation have come under the searchlight of the critical segment of the Nigerian polity. Among the issues that have brought negative publicity to the Nigeria Police today are the failed (coup) attempt in Anambra State by which unscrupulous but brazen politicians attempted to remove a democratically elected governor, using senor elements of the Nigeria Police, the allegations of massive fraud and habitual extortion against the highest authorities in the Nigeria Police, as well as a recent report that junior officers in a Police Command in Osun State carried placards to protest the exorbitant financial returns that were being demanded of them daily by superior officers.

Nigerians are all too familiar with the daily extortion of motorists on our roads - at regular checkpoints and illegal roadblocks. So, the allegation of the junior officers may not be far from the truth. These days road travellers encounter no less than twenty emergency checkpoints between Lagos and Ibadan, and at each one of these points, commercial bus drivers and taxis have (as a matter of routine) to part with N20.00. The practice is the same nearly everywhere in the country. And there is no camouflage about it. The toll is demanded and collected openly by the men in uniform with the aid of their firearms. And the drivers do invariably comply, as under those circumstances only a mad man can begin to question an officer with a loaded AK 47 rifle. Many times in the past, drivers or conductors have allegedly been shot dead for refusing or delaying to pay the illegal toll demanded by gun-toting officers on the road.

Apart from the widespread extortion that is associated with the Police in this country, the officers and men often operate like an aberrant order, intimidating, coercing and brutalising Nigerian citizens in total disregard for all constitutional provisions regarding the limits of their powers or the rights of citizens. There has not been any marked difference in operational style between the Colonial Police Force that was put together for the sole purpose of subjugating the Nigerian people or coercing them into submission, and the post-Independence Nigeria Police. Perhaps no conscious efforts have been made since independence to transform the Nigeria Police into a civil agency that is aimed at maintaining order and protecting lives and property.

Thus, for the slightest misdemeanour they often deal with "bloody civilians" in the bloodiest manner. At Police Stations, at public functions, and at regular checkpoints or emergency roadblocks, they are known to have harassed, extorted, brutalised and tortured innocent Nigerians mercilessly. What is more, trigger-happy police officers are alleged to have often shot innocent people and framed up charges of armed robbery against their dead victims in order to escape the law. And perpetrators of these dastardly acts have nearly always escaped punishment as Nigerian relations of such victims are often too ignorant, too poor or too frightened of the police to take up the prosecution of the matter decisively.

One only needs to see the Mobile Squad or the Anti-Riot Police at work to recognise that perhaps they are not trained to keep the law, but rather to "kill and go." They have often deployed tanks and armoured personnel carriers and used live bullets to suppress students' demonstrations or the peaceful demonstration of workers on the occasion of a labour strike. The senseless carnage during the recent labour strike over the fuel price increase is still fresh in our memory. Police officers who accompany rich men and women or top government officials and their wives in escort vehicles, and those of them who accompany cash-carrying bullion vans, are often armed with guns, clubs and horsewhips, with which they whip and bash fellow citizens out of the road. The recklessness with which they drive their siren-blaring vehicles, and the brute force and bravado with which they send other road users off the highway whenever they are passing, constitute nothing but a reign of terror. This is why in the perception of many Nigerians; the Police Officer is far from being "a friend." No wonder the younger segment of our society has come to see the police as their foremost enemy, and a target for the visitation of vengeance during any of our crisis situations.

One of the most fundamental responsibilities of government is the protection of lives and property and the safeguarding of law and order in society. The Police constitute the principal agents for the carrying out of this important responsibility of state. Yet there must be certain laws and regulations that guide the conduct of the police. The Nigerian elite must now begin to ask: What are the rights and limitations of the Police before the citizens? What are the rights and limitations of the citizens before the Police? Even when dealing with crime suspects, the Police is not given a blank cheque. There are numerous international conventions regarding the fundamental human rights of suspects, who must be presumed innocent until they are proven guilty through the due process of law. Nigeria is a signatory to many of these conventions.

We have the Constitution of the Federal Republic of Nigeria. We also have the Police Ordinance and the Police Act. But which law permits the Nigeria Police to parade mere suspects before TV cameras as we see every day in our country? How is it that the authorities of our NTA and other Television stations do not see anything wrong in parading mere suspects before the whole world and declaring them "armed robbers" before any charges are instituted against them? Which law permits the police to kill or as they say *waste* criminal suspects or those alleged to be armed robbers? Officers and men of the Panti Police Station in Lagos are notorious for executing armed robbery suspects right there in the station. Do the authorities pretend not to know of the murderous activities of these Police Officers in Panti and elsewhere in the country? Which law permits the officers and men of the regular Police who mount roadblocks to harass or brutalise road users with arms and ammunition purchased at public expense? Which law permits a military officer, a government official or a cash-carrying bank chief, or simply a rich man, to force other road users off the public highway with sirens, loaded guns and horsewhips?

The conduct of our Police Officers in Nigeria has not only legal but also moral implications for us. To whatever extent the allegations against officers of the Nigeria Police are correct, there are ethical or moral issues that are involved in the intimidation and extortion of innocent Nigerians. There are ethical or moral issues involved in the brutalising and killing of Nigerians by those who are paid to secure their lives and property. Today any rich Nigerian can go to the District Police Officer and pay for any number of Policemen to guard him at home or accompany him on a journey. Such a rich Nigerian could actually keep a detachment of Policemen permanently for his personal security, so long as the officer in charge is paid. But there are ethical or moral issues involved in this widespread privatisation of the police by rich Nigerians or Nigerians holding political office at a particular time. How shall we overcome the present perceived state of anomie and immorality in the conduct of the Nigeria Police?

I am continually puzzled by the fact that Nigerians who have become notorious among the nations of the world for monumental corruption, can also find a place among the most religious people in the modern world. Is it not true that the majority of our Police officers and men are either Christians or Muslims? Is it not true that the degenerate Nigeria Policemen and women are among those who fill the Mosques on Friday and the Churches on Sunday? Can't those of them who have pretensions to religiosity see the contradiction between their weekend piety and their weekday deceit, extortion and brutality? Where is the link between faith and life? What are the moral imperatives of their ritual practice? What are the ethical implications of their professional conduct? What has happened to the conscience of the average Nigerian in or out of uniform?

True, the Nigeria Police may be terribly corrupt. But they are only a measure of the Nigerian degenerate environment. The conduct of the April 2003 general elections and the ugly fallouts of that exercise that was nothing short of a national reproach, are a testimony to the disconnect between the moral values associated with Christianity and Islam, and the corrupt lifestyle of the majority of Nigerians. So, what has happened to our sense of right and wrong, good and evil, fair and foul? What we are seeing today appears to be a damning verdict on religious bodies and their preoccupation in this country. Perhaps Christian and Muslim leaders in this country have been so preoccupied with the politics of religion that they have neglected to build in their individual members a truly religious conscience. Perhaps religious leaders have been carried away by the illusion of numbers, such that at the end of the day, while their churches and mosques are filled to capacity and in spite of so much noise and fanfare, the generality of Nigerians are yet to know the God of truth, justice and love.

CHAPTER EIGHTEEN

Politics and the Manipulation of Religion in Nigeria
(Written on September 15, 2003)

Religion features at the very beginning of our nation's constitution. In the preamble to the 1999 Nigerian constitution, it is affirmed that we intend to live together as one united country under God. Indeed, the overwhelming majority of Nigerians are religious people. We believe in the supremacy of God. We believe that God is the very basis of our individual lives and our corporate existence. We believe in and relate with supernatural realities through prayers and supplications and through the offering of sacrifices. We find churches, mosques, shrines and sundry prayer houses everywhere in the land. We take part in crusades, worship sessions and vigils; we offer sacrifices and observe fasting days and religious holidays; and we go in large numbers on religious pilgrimages to Jerusalem and Mecca, taking pride in being called Jerusalem Pilgrim (JP) or Alhaji the rest of our lives.

While there is noticeable decline in religious fervour in many parts of the world, the religious enterprise appears to be thriving very much in Nigeria, as more and more company warehouses and private buildings are being converted to prayer houses, and our sports stadia all over the country are being used more for religious crusades than for sporting events. Streets within our towns and villages, as well as inter-state highways are often blocked these days by enthusiastic worshippers who flock to churches and camp meetings. In many of our urban areas, there are as many churches and mosques as there are streets! In an article that appeared last year in New York Times (March 13, 2002), the writer, one Norimitsu Onishi noted that "Christianity is growing faster in sub-Saharan Africa than in any other place on earth. Roman Catholicism and the major protestant denominations are gaining more followers every day, but new churches are leading the boom."

In the last few years, a new dimension has also been added to the thriving religious enterprise. It is the increased patronage of high-ranking public officials who not only openly call for and sponsor regular prayer sessions in different prayer houses but have themselves become born again Christians and prayer merchants, often appearing at church crusades and prayer vigils with all the paraphernalia of public office, and sometimes grabbing the microphone to deliver sanctimonious homilies and earth-shaking prayers. At the end of last year, the Christmas carol service at the state house chapel in Abuja, which lasted several hours, was televised live on national television. And to usher in the New Year, Governor Ahmed Tinubu, himself a Muslim, had the Christian chapel he built in the Lagos state house dedicated with much religious fanfare. This gesture paid off for him, as many Christians contributed their votes to see that Tinubu retained the governorship at the April 19, 2003, elections.

President Obasanjo and a number of Christian governors have thriving chapels at the State House where prayer meetings, morning devotions, night vigils and praise worship sessions are regularly held to storm heaven and intercede for the nation and its leaders. There are palace prophets and priests who are engaged full time at the state house chapels to pray for the chief executive, drive demons away from him, to curse or call for fire and brimstone over the enemies of progress who may be making life difficult for the chief executive who God has anointed over his people. The palace prophets often lose sight of any prophetic dimension to their ministry, and become part and parcel of the regime, prodding the leader on, and assuring him that all shall be well, even when the rest of us can see that he is sitting on a pack of cards.

These days, prayer and preaching sessions are no longer limited to churches, mosques and homes. They are held at corporate boardrooms, in government offices, in commercial buses and in open markets. Nigerians going about their daily business can be seen brandishing the Bible or the Koran, the Rosary or Islamic prayer beads. The largest billboards in our towns and cities are those advertising upcoming religious crusades and faith healing carnivals. Religious exclamations such as "to God be the glory," "praise the Lord," and "Allahu Akbar," are often on the lips of Nigerians, at work or at play - from the exalted members of the National Executive Council or Council of State to the young ones who are about to sit Common Entrance examination. Thus, Nigerians are a chronically religious people. The whole environment is awash with religiosity. No wonder today's leaders have found it so easy to manipulate religion for political gains. While many critical Nigerians today see Obasanjo as a callous, vindictive and power-drunk dictator who was ready to compromise every principle in the book to stay put in power, he proclaims himself as a born-again Christian, and many Christian pastors have been dancing around him and proclaiming him as the messiah God has sent to save this country from disintegration.

While anti-corruption crusaders have accused many prominent politicians, including Senate President Pius Anyim of corrupt enrichment, these same politicians were always welcome at major Pentecostal Crusades where they often mounted the rostrum and took over the preaching from the pastor. Critical social commentators might have considered former Minister of Information, Professor Jerry Gana a shallow propagandist who was always available to do the dirty job for President Obasanjo, but he was a high-level minister in his church, and he justified everything he did with the fact that he was acting for God. And Governor Nnamani is alleged to be killing his people every day, but he appears on TV with the slogan "to God be the glory." The list of born-again Christians in government is endless. Yet Nigerian politics is dirty, and the environment stinks with corruption. Is what we have simply the manipulation of religion for political ends?

CHAPTER NINETEEN

Youth Restiveness, Social Instability and the Quest for Peace in a Democratic Nigeria
(Written on December 11, 2003)

Youth restiveness and social instability have become a major source of concern for many Nigerians, who, through the years of debauchery under the military had hoped and prayed and looked forward to peace and security at the termination of the evil dispensation. But rather than experience peace and security, we are today confronted more than ever before with the tenuous nature of our national polity and the frightening dimensions that youth restiveness and social instability have assumed in Nigeria.

From the sporadic exploits of the bloodthirsty sharia zealots of the North West and North Central Region, to the incessant display of violence by the angry mafia of the Niger Delta Region, and from the armed bandits that rule the highways of the North East, to the hired assassins that paint the political landscape in the South East with blood, and from the hot-headed ethnic militia known as the O.P.C in the South West and MASSOB in the South East, to the murderous secret cultists in nearly all our universities and polytechnics, it has been an orgy of violence and a season of blood and tears in which the very foundation of the nation is now threatened. Precious human lives have been destroyed in their thousands, and property worth hundreds of millions of Naira have been set ablaze in Odi, Warri, Lagos, Shagamu, Aguleri, Umuleri, Ife, Modakeke, ZakiBiam, Kaduna, Kano, Bauchi, Jos, and lately Abuja. We have witnessed thousands of internally displaced persons or refugees squatting in police and army barracks all over the place.

We have been through a season of madness here in Nigeria, and individuals and groups have often taken care of their own security by hiring police escorts, constituting vigilante groups or even forming private armies which operated largely outside the law. To combat the growing crime in our cities, some state governments constituted terrorist squads that were worse than the notorious "kill and go" arm of the police force. These killer squads often adopted such code names as "Operation Sweep," "Operation Crush," Operation Wedge," "Operation Flush" and "Operation Fire for Fire." They were often mandated to shoot suspects at sight, and they often did their job with utmost recklessness. We would never know the number of innocent Nigerians who have been sent to their early graves as a result of the activities of these state-sponsored bandits. The young people of Nigeria have been growing up in this jungle and watching the Hobbesian existence that we call life – nasty, brutish and short. Our young people have been learning and playing out the jungle law of the survival of the fittest, and Nigeria is the worse for it.

Today the youths of the Niger Delta are at war with the Federal Government, with the Oil Companies and with one another, killing, abducting, maiming, raping and harassing innocent people. From Bori to Eleme and from Bomadi to Warri, the impression is that no one is in control. Instead, what we are confronted with is total lawlessness or anarchy. In Lagos too the youth wing of the Oodua Peoples Congress has been credited with several killings at various locations in the city at various times. We are all familiar with the violent exploits of the "Area Boys" who command the streets of our major cities, harassing, extorting and terrorizing members of the public. Thus, it appears that through all the years of debauchery, when the military held reign, incalculable damage has been done to the psyche of the Nigerian youth. They no longer seem to be able to distinguish between good and bad, between virtue and vice, and between right and wrong. They seem to have lost faith in the adult society, in the leadership and even in their parents and teachers.

How indeed could the young people have learnt the lesson on the sanctity of life when daily they heard of adults and children being kidnapped, killed and dismembered for ritual purposes by members of the adult society? How could they have come to appreciate the truth of the inviolability of life when daily they were confronted with the reality of human corpses that are left to decompose and decapitate on our streets, while thousands of people passed by and only blocked their noses against the stench? How could our young people have accepted that violence is evil when everyday they watched the rich and powerful crush the poor and lowly with all the instruments of violence at their disposal, and when such criminals were treated as successful members of society? How could they have accepted the truth of human transcendence when they heard that government agents were sometimes involved in the sordid conspiracy that we call ritual murder?

How can you demonstrate to our young people that human life is not cheap, expendable, and disposable when (in the absence of a truly functional film censorship body) even the youngest and the most vulnerable among them are exposed to the most outrageous celebration of violence on TV by way of home videos? How can they accept the rule of law and respect the rights and freedoms of their neighbours, when everyday they watch innocent people humiliated, tortured and eliminated, while the culprits who are often well connected, go scot-free? How can our young people be made to value human life and respect the rights and dignity of persons when their leaders and elders have demonstrated to them that wealth and power are the ultimate values, when these leaders and elders would stop at nothing in the pursuit of these values, when they would blackmail, kidnap, torture or even eliminate anyone who may be in their way to the acquisition of maximum wealth and power? How can they accept that secret cults are bad when they observe that access to wealth and position is often guaranteed and safe passage through the corridors of power is often secured through one's enlistment in one of such adult cults as the Ogboni Confraternity or the Rosicrucians?

How can you make the young people in our schools and colleges sit down and concentrate on their studies when the leaders have messed up the educational set-up to such an extent that universities have been shut on many occasions for upward of six months, and there was no provision for any profitable engagement of their young minds during the period? Do we not say that the devil makes use of the idle mind? How can our students be eager to study, to pass their examinations and to graduate from the university, when there are no jobs awaiting them, when even for the mandatory Youth Service Scheme they sometimes have to bribe their way to be able to find placement, after having been deployed to such places as Lagos, Abuja, Port Harcourt and Warri? How can they value life amidst acrimonious poverty, when many young people are reduced to a state of destitution, when they are made to struggle with malnourishment, and when they have to study in an environment that is degenerate and decrepit, while they watch in amazement the conspicuous consumption of those who have stolen food off their hands?

True, we have not given our young people reason to live with dignity and responsibility. We have often been the cause of our young people's restiveness. It has been observed that "when life is worthless, fear is banished." Young people are highly impressionable. They easily take scandal. They can easily be led astray. It is only by practical example from members of the adult society that they will learn that the fear of God is the beginning of wisdom; that human life is sacred, unique and inviolable; and that money, power and position are not the highest values for which other values may be so easily sacrificed.

Thus, after years of military dictatorship, the worst form of which was manifested in the Abacha dispensation, Nigerians had hoped for a period of peaceful transition to a just, equitable, democratic, and peaceful society. We had hoped for a new Nigerian society where we can once again have the opportunity to channel our enormous natural endowments to positive use for the advancement of our teeming population. We had hoped for a new Nigerian society where we can celebrate the richness of our diverse languages, cultures and religions. We had hoped for a new Nigerian society where we can take our rightful place in the comity of nations and compete in the advancement of science and technology. But rather than make progress in these directions, multiple crises and conflicts have plagued post-military Nigeria.

As a result of these sad developments, the Nigerian economy remains comatose. Investors have been scared away, in spite of President Obasanjo's numerous overseas travels, and in spite of successfully hosting the 8th All African Games and the Commonwealth Heads of Governments Meeting. With the circumstance of widespread violence and great insecurity in the land, potential investors seem to have decided to watch and see. Unemployment therefore remains high and the majority of the people are plagued by acrimonious poverty, with the lot of the youth population worsening by the day. Thus, four and a half years after we said goodbye to military dictatorship, we are witnessing what appears sadly as another round of aborted dreams, broken promises and dashed hopes. Once again, our leaders have failed to deliver, and we are once again being challenged to go to the drawing board.

The unfortunate turn of events in the last four and a half years surely brings to the fore the reality of our tenuous existence, the restiveness of our youth, in and out of school, and the imperative of social reconstruction towards national reconciliation and peaceful co-existence.

This social reconstruction necessarily involves an ethical or moral revolution, the type that religious groups are best equipped to champion and promote. Perhaps the people of Nigeria along with their leaders had underestimated the extent of the problems that had built up in the land over the years of debauchery, when systemic corruption, social injustice, economic isolation and political banditry reigned, breeding widespread anger and resentment that were kept in check all the while only by military might. With the violent conflicts that have erupted in the North and South, and in the East and West, over unresolved ethnic, religious, political and economic differences, and over boundaries and the ownership of land and other resources, Nigerians must now realise that there are lots of structural defects in the Nigerian society that are a potential source of conflict. With our universities and colleges becoming breeding grounds for gangsters and murderers, perhaps the time has come for us to look critically at the very structure of our corporate existence, the management of our natural and human resources and what our developmental priorities are. This is a challenge we must take up and address courageously, perhaps, as many have suggested, in a national conference.

The truth I have come to recognise is that many in the Igbo nation remain resentful of the rest of Nigeria for the injustices of the 1967 to 1970 civil war, the abandoned property imbroglio, and the alleged post-war marginalisation of Igbo people in some vital segments of the national economy. These are the sentiments behind the Movement for the Actualisation of the Sovereign State of Biafra (MASSOB). Many in the Yoruba nation remain angry with the rest of Nigeria for the injustices associated with the June 12 election annulment, and the alleged post-June 12 persecution and marginalisation of Yoruba people. These are the sentiments that sustain the activities of the Oodua Peoples Congress. The collocation of small ethnic nationalities which we call the Middle Belt are today vexed by the appendage status accorded them in the power structures of our nation. Many of them allege that they have suffered numerous injustices because of being falsely associated with the North all this time, while they gained nothing from the Northern hold on political power. These are the sentiments behind the activities of the Middle Belt Forum.

The citizens of the oil producing Niger Delta are poised for a showdown with the rest of Nigeria, and if recent clashes are anything to go by, their youths appear to be well equipped for war with the rest of Nigeria, because of the callous exploitation of their natural resources for decade, while they are abandoned in a state of destitution. The Egbesu Youth best exemplify these sentiments. Many among the Hausa and Fulani Muslims of the core North who desire to live under the supremacy of the Islamic Sharia seem incensed that the rest of Nigeria wants to jettison what they see as their religious freedom. These are the sentiments behind the 2000, 2001 and 2002 religious riots that rocked Kaduna, Kano and Jos. Within each group however, there is often bitterness over past hurts and wounds which have never been seriously addressed.

The orgy of violence all over the place and the restiveness of youth amidst our fledgling democracy may be an expression of the failure of state and the collapse of governance. There is nothing on the ground to demonstrate that ours is not a land run over by political bandits, ethnic warlords and religious fanatics. That is why the average citizen now seems to have lost confidence in the capacity of those in power to protect their lives and property. With a selfless, visionary and prudent leadership, the thousands of deaths we have recorded and the millions of Naira worth of property that have been destroyed in the last few years, could have been avoided. So we hold the current leadership of the Nigerian State responsible for the restiveness of the youth and the widespread violence and social instability that have resulted, because the leaders have remained indolent and insensitive in the face of very explosive situations.

With so many un-addressed wounds and hurts over past injustices and inequities, and with corruption having assumed epidemic dimension, our leaders have often carried on business as usual, dining and wining, taking chieftaincy titles and honorary degrees and conferring the highest national honours on themselves. But for serious-minded Nigerians, the task of nation-building must begin with an elaborate programme of, and an honest commitment to social reconstruction and moral revolution as the first steps towards peaceful co-existence, or else our preoccupation with democratic governance will lack the much-needed foundation, and end once again in disaster. Instead of squandering our meagre resources on prestige projects and looking for every available opportunity to play the big brother to neighbouring countries and give lavish receptions to international visitors, the leadership of Nigeria must learn to feel the pulse of the nation, to hear the cry of the people, and to react with utmost sense of responsibility to the desires and aspirations of the constituent units of the country for that kind of unity and peace that is based on mutual forgiveness for past hurts and wounds, and a mutual commitment to righting the wrongs of the past, and building our society on the principles of transparency, justice, fairness, and a passion among the leaders for the common good.

Before Nigeria collapses under the burden of monumental corruption, long-standing mutual antipathy, and violent conflicts, we hereby challenge peace-desiring Nigerians to champion the cause of national reconstruction through the promotion of the much needed moral and ethical revolution on the one hand, and a heavy investment in conflict resolution, the rehabilitation of our educational institutions and the provision of employment opportunities for the teeming population of our young people on the other.

We challenge the members of the Laity Council of Nigeria and indeed all Nigerian Christians to do an examination of conscience, and to take up the challenge of this moral revolution and national reconstruction. Members of the Laity Council must heed the wake-up call now, if there must begin a process of emancipation from a blighted future to which unborn generations seem to be condemned. We must develop a cohesive network for the incremental engagement of the nation's leadership on national issues, drawing on the sectoral specialisation of the members of the Laity Council across the country to educate and lead the masses.

The issue of impropriety in governance for example, whether in relation to electoral or constitutional manipulation, corrupt financial dealings in the Assemblies or such exploits as the celebrated Anambra state gubernatorial debacle, can be appropriately tackled by a group of Catholic Lawyers, acting as the arrowhead of civil society action, closely supported by an alert and committed independent press. And we cannot act alone. It is not possible to achieve the desired national transformation in isolation. We must seek out committed Nigerians and work assiduously to form and strengthen coalitions among such people across ethnic and even religious boundaries. As Church we must see ourselves as the light of the world. We must champion this noble cause of national transformation, for where there is no vision, the people perish.

CHAPTER TWENTY

State Failure: The Inevitability of Change
(Written on March 29, 2004)

In recent times our lives in Nigeria have been dominated by acrimonious poverty and a worsening security situation, with widespread violence in the form of armed robbery, arson and politically motivated assassinations. Ours remains a country with a depressed economy, where millions are under-nourished, where economic and social infrastructures are collapsing and tottering despite heavy re-investment, where the numbers of employable but unemployed graduates and other categories of young people are mounting yearly and no jobs are forthcoming, where educational institutions experience long closures and admission into them continually hangs in the balance, and where our health delivery system remains stagnant.

In clear contrast to this national scenario is a political leadership class that wallows in conspicuous consumption and social self-adulation, as they declare national carnivals now and again like the gladiators of old to celebrate the purchase of new chieftaincy titles, new national honours or new honorary doctorate degrees. No wonder then that in these convoluted times, many of our youths are taking to crime, hiring themselves out as thugs and assassins for the same rulers whose responsibility it is to direct their energies and talents to positive ends. No wonder our students are indulging more and more in cultism and perfecting the language and culture of the underworld. No wonder our notoriety is growing with the most intuitive scammers in our climes.

Balanced against our endowment and potential, our circumstance of humiliation in this country today suggests the failure of the state apparatus and those who preside over it. To put it mildly, we have no visionary leadership in place. Instead, evidence abounds that what leadership we have is simply self-serving and opportunistic. With the reality on the ground today where the masses are more and more depressed in all sectors, the gap is ever widening between them and a leadership feeding fat and getting richer by the day, a leadership enjoying self-awarded perquisites, a leadership whose wards are often comfortably ensconced in foreign lands. Only yesterday, many of these professional political parasites were out there, gaunt and hungry like the rest of us, bemoaning their lean fortunes. But today they have metamorphosed into deities who are no longer sharing the pains of the ordinary people in the land and who cannot understand why the people should cry.

An overview of recent happenings leaves little on our national horizon to cheer about, but merely reinforces the concern being expressed by serious minded citizens and cynics alike that Nigeria is in a state of anomie and perilously on a merry-go-round. Our national disaster has been in the making and has been nourished on virtually all segments by a pedestrian leadership that the good people of this nation do not deserve. The shame and national embarrassment that was the March 27 local government elections, and the spate of arson and politically motivated killings that preceded and attended that exercise all over the country, are a graphic statement on the security status and the perilous political climate of this country. Yet the leadership is unscathed and remains entrenched in comfortable positions.

Lawlessness even in high places and the brazen escapades of political kingpins now invade and intrude the political life of the high and mighty, threatening to undermine national security and entrench banditry as a political culture. Whole sections of our highways have virtually been bought over by bandits who now operate freely, sporadically terrorising, robbing, killing and traumatizing road users. While these dastardly acts are perpetuated, our police are conveniently out of sight, busy elsewhere enthusiastically collecting illegal toll fees for themselves and their masters.

Nigerians are hardly ever known to quit public positions on grounds of failure, incompetence, neglect, scandal or moral integrity. Even in the face of obvious neglect and mismanagement of public resources, it is not in our character to quit the stage, and when occasionally forced to do so following rotten scandals our leaders are let off the hook to flaunt their ill-gotten gains and to worm their way back to political relevance at various levels, using the same ill-gotten wealth to buy up the people.

But our situation is not irredeemable. We are not bound to put up with rogue leadership forever. Nigerians are not a different breed of human beings from citizens elsewhere such as in Singapore or Malaysia, South Africa or Ghana. Many of us believe that Nigeria is not impossible to govern. Many believe that a major factor in the leadership conundrum is the question of the moral credentials of those who have volunteered to lead us, and who occupy positions of power, whether by fair or foul means. Their true motive is often not to serve the people of this country but to take advantage of the prevailing political contradictions and economic distress for personal aggrandisement. Consequently, the average Nigerian political leader develops an imperial air of condescension and once in power treats the people with utter disrespect, sometimes bordering on contempt and disdain.

The government of the day is insensitive to the yearnings of the people. It has often turned a deaf ear to their cry of desperation. Those who are holding the reins of power believe too much in themselves, as if they know it all and have everything in control. In their own eyes they are doing wonderfully well, but the signals everywhere are that this government has lost its bearing, it has failed woefully. Yet, before such an insensitive government, the people appear to have resigned to fate, praying as usual that the heavens will intervene. But if this country must make any headway, if the progressive decay in the polity must be halted, if the descent into anarchy in Nigeria must be averted, if a people's revolution is to be forestalled, then change in the character of governance is inevitable and urgent. And we shall need to accompany our prayer with action to bring it about.

We need a paradigm shift from a reactive to a proactive citizenry, and from an apathetic populace to a community of popular participation in governance, where the paths to public service are not as smooth and attractive as they are now for feudal lords, rogues, thieves and brigands, and where the gains of office even for an inept crop of leaders are not as rewarding as they are currently fashioned out to be. We need a shift in leadership character and focus sustained by transparency and accountability where civil society will engage the political leadership in balancing policy objectives against concrete acts of governance.

The generality of the Nigerian people who have had to put up with a succession of rogue leaders and whose sensibilities are today continually insulted by punitive overlords in the corridors of power, shall need to wake up from their slumber and reaffirm their belief in the sovereign power of the people. Civil society shall have to shake off its shackles and break out of the political inertia in which it presently finds itself and redefine the character of leadership for the Nigerian nation. The desired change will come about when civil society rejects the unfolding ignominious political system that is driven by a lack of moral credibility on the part of politicians who got into power with questionable electoral credentials. The desired change will come about when civil society identifies and rejects the political parasites who are isolated and alienated from the social circumstance of the people, and who do not share in the economic austerity of the moment but whose interests lie in feeding on the tears of the people.

It does not take a soothsayer to recognise that Nigeria is today floundering on a precipice with the palpable danger of a fatal crash landing. A leadership that is hell-bent on taxing the poor masses to the bone materially and psychologically as the only way to fulfil promises of providing any measure of relief for them will end up taxing the patience of an already drained populace. The country can only take so much of rogue leadership. Time is running out. Current leaders and aspirants to leadership will do well to read the signs of the times and heed the admonition for change in leadership style and character while the day still lasts.

True, Nigerians at the grassroots may not yet have reached the revolutionary sophistication of dealing with leaders who have stolen, rigged or intimidated their way into power, but this situation should not be misread, for neither the leaders nor their acolytes would be spared should the masses suddenly cultivate the appetite for genuine social, political and economic freedom. It will indeed be a costly mistake to tax the legendary resilience of the people to the breaking point. Time is running out for our leaders. But if today our leaders undergo the much-needed conversion and toe the line of sanity, they may yet wean the people from the inevitable option of a popular revolt.

CHAPTER TWENTY ONE

It's Leadership, Stupid!
(Written on November 10, 2004)

I have had two major opportunities for international exposure and training this year. In the month of May I was in far-away Canberra, Australia, studying the dynamics of Christian Covenant Communities, and I came off with a rich experience that I believe will enhance my life and ministry. But while studying in Canberra, the Australian capital city, I took note of the environmental beauty, the structural order and the neatness of the city. I was particularly impressed by the way Canberra (unlike many modern cities), is full of parks, gardens and massive woodlands. Rather than a concrete jungle like you have in Sydney the old capital city, Canberra boasts of shady groves, tall trees and gorgeous hedges lining the major streets. About 50 years ago, the Australian government saw that Sydney was becoming congested and they decided to develop a new capital city in Canberra, located between Sydney and Melbourne. They had a vision to make Canberra one of the most beautiful cities in the world and they have supported this vision with necessary policies and legislations which successive leaders seem passionately committed to.

I savoured the beauty of this city and wondered whether any Nigerian leader has ever visited this place. But my joy soon turned sour when I was informed that Canberra is actually one of the 73 cities all over the world visited by Nigerian leaders and experts when they were planning to build up Abuja as the new capital city. See what mess Nigerians have made of Abuja! Did our leaders and experts close their eyes when they visited Canberra and such other beautiful places in the world? What did they learn from the various modern settlements they visited? What kind of human beings do we have hanging around our own corridors of power?

Once again in the month of October I was spending my leave participating at an advanced leadership training programme in the Haggai Institute located in Singapore. It was an intensely packed course dealing with skills, methodologies and paradigms in leadership, and facilitated by some of the best experts in the field. I learnt a lot from the training programme. I believe that I am a little better equipped to respond to the many challenges that face all categories of leaders in an increasingly complex human society. I am looking forward to sharing my experiences with colleagues in the Church and in the Nigerian civil society as we all grapple with and strive to overcome the messy socio-economic and political circumstances which a succession of visionless leaders have led Nigeria into.

While in Singapore I took some time to look around, read books and ask questions on how such a tiny island that is devoid of natural resources became such a developmental phenomenon, and I kept wondering why resource rich Nigeria should remain such a backward and beggarly nation after 44 years of independence. Singapore occupies a tiny island off the tip of the Malaysian Peninsula and has a population of about 8 million. It started out slightly behind Nigeria, gaining independence by force of circumstance from Britain in 1965, and in under 40 years building an empire of superlative proportions. Today it prides itself of being the cleanest state in the world. It has an efficient airline and a sparkling airport, as is its skyline at night. It operates visa-free entry for visitors from Commonwealth countries, and it has order, efficiency, control and courtesy. It has about the largest container shipping port in the world.

With no crude oil of its own, Singapore's petroleum refining facilities are among the best and most efficient in the world. Of nations nurtured and sustained entirely on tourism, Singapore counts among the best in the world. From its waking moment to the end of each passing day, Singapore runs an economy anchored on tourism with other arteries of activity equally contributing to a national economy that generates one of the highest per capita incomes in the world.

With practically no natural resource to count on apart from its human population, Singapore is simply a miracle of human ingenuity and enterprise at work. The small island state is surrounded by sea water. It has no rivers, no springs and no fresh water. So it imports water from Malaysia. With no natural beaches of its own, it developed its exotic artificial beaches with imported sand. Its underwater world of aquatic tourist attraction is quite a sight to behold.

The success story that Singapore exemplifies is a success story of visionary leadership. It is about an individual or a group of individuals cultivating and harnessing their inspirational instincts for development. It is about harvesting and channelling economic gains for the common good. Attracting, trapping and tapping external resources to a resource-barren environment for the realization of such high development objectives became an obsession for Lee Kwan Yew, the highly controversial but agreeably charismatic, courageous and purpose-driven founding father and architect of modern Singapore and his immediate collaborators.

Realising such national development goals of any nation demands sterling qualities and unwavering commitment of the leadership. Along the way, distractive elements such as corruption, lawlessness and indiscipline have to be confronted and neutralized. They have no place in a country hungry enough for development. It is said and is indeed true that people are often able to be carried to as far a height as leaders are willing and courageous enough to carry them. In a society or organisation, the combination of people, ideas, resources and time makes up a basket of the potential force available and capable of propelling it.

The overwhelming majority of a citizenry, perhaps 90%, are in this category that watch things happen and get mildly involved. At the bottom of the pile (about 5%) are the group that neither knows nor cares that things happen and so they do not get involved. But at the top (the critical 5%) are the leaders, the catalytic agents that make things happen, that activate the latent force in society. That is the segment that Lee Kwan Yew championed for the transformation of Singapore which in 1965 had little chance of survival as a nation, but which today is rated among the most developed countries of the world. The leader is thus the defining factor in the pace and direction at which an entire group moves and is thus critical to the degree of success or failure of the group's fortunes.

This is the phenomenon that Singapore has so graphically illustrated in its development profile. It is a nation building on its yesterday and tending its today for tomorrow. This is why, without any natural resources whatsoever, it has developed the structures that have helped it to weather the storm of racial crisis in the late 1960s and the more recent threat of the SARS epidemic to its tourism industry. This is why developing an economically viable process of desalinating sea water to reduce dependence on importation of fresh water is currently high on the national agenda. This is why the country has developed elaborate economic imperatives and incentives to sustain stability and growth. This is why young Singaporean adults gladly and proudly give two and a half years of military service to their country and why the young people are currently challenged to come up with ideas on their vision for an even greater Singapore.

We cannot take anything away from Singaporeans and what they have made of their small island state. We cannot but note with admiration the giant strides they have made towards becoming a socio-economic beehive in Asia and on a global scale. We cannot but applaud the single-minded devotion to national development that has seen a third world country become a first world country in one generation. Singaporeans are a mixture of Asiatic cultures that have blended into a vibrant population of hard-working citizens who are proud of what their country has achieved.

Back at home we have spent ourselves bemoaning our lot in a land richly blessed with people, ideas, resources and time. We have agonised over how, in spite of all these gifts, we are rooted to the starting blocks where we started the post-independence development race with societies such as Singapore. We may try the escapist approach by pointing to our sheer size and complexities, but 'Singapore' can be replicated in many places to give a coherent national mosaic. As long as we remain saddled with visionless leadership, corrupt leadership, leadership without moral principles, leadership without responsibility and leadership without discipline, so long shall we remain a bumbling giant holding only a basket of potential force.

As long as our leaders aspire to positions of power without any clear-cut vision and programme for their constituency, so long shall we remain in our sorry state. As long as our leaders assume unwholesome power without any sense of commitment to the common good, and without the disposition to go out there and lead by example, so long shall they be consigned to the scrap heap of history. Lee Kuan Yew and others will forever remain the shining stars of Singapore. He may have been seen to be dictatorial and tough-handed in some of his approaches to realising the national vision, but have we not had our own dose of dictatorship? And where did it lead us except that ours was heavily laced with corruption, mediocrity and ineptitude.

Singapore has been blessed with charismatic, visionary, selfless and courageous leaders with a passion for the common good and a commitment to excellence, but Nigeria has been plagued by a succession of visionless, punitive, selfish and klemptocratic rulers! And so when we look at Singapore and such other countries and we wring our hands and wonder what in the world is the matter with us and our country, and why such places are so blessed and we are in such dire state, the answer now appears to me very simple: The miracle of Singapore is the curse of Nigeria – It's leadership, stupid!

CHAPTER TWENTY TWO

Democracy and the Culture of Impunity in Nigeria
(Written on December 14, 2004)

A mong the fundamental objectives of governance in a modern state is the maintenance of law and order or the protection of lives and property. The modern democratic state is one ruled not by the whims and caprices of the ruler, no matter how wise the ruler may be, and much less by a powerful oligarchy, but by the constitution of the land which binds everyone equally. The modern state is organised in such a way and equipped with such public spirited security apparatus that the citizens are never at any time at the mercy of petty criminals and paid thugs and touts; they never have to sleep with one eye open for fear of political bandits and paid thugs and touts; they never have to run for dear life at the mention of religious fanatics and ethnic warlords; they never have to stay indoors for fear of secret cultists and area boys. Yes, in organised modern societies where the rule of law is in place, governors and their families do not have to take oaths before juju priests in the middle of the night, nor do they have to flee the state house now and again at the instance of hired assassins and godfathers of primitive feudalism.

Since the emergence of the present democratic dispensation, Nigerians have witnessed too many instances of not only acts of lawlessness in high and low places, but what may be described as anomie or even impunity. From the Presidency which could order the destruction of Odi and ZakiBiam villages in revenge for the killing of officers of the Nigerian Army and the police, to the National Assembly members who openly asked for bribe before endorsing ministerial candidates, and from the illegal checkpoints daily mounted by policeman on the road who, armed with his AK 47 extorts money from transporters in broad daylight, to the customs officer at our air and seaports who demands bribery from those bringing goods into the country, without looking back; and from the LASTMA operatives to the

Area Boys on the streets of Lagos who openly intimidate and extort road users, the impression is that no one is in control.

Two years ago, Nigeria lost its Minister of Justice and Attorney General, Chief Bola Ige in the most brutal circumstances, and till today, there are no clues. Once upon a time the chief suspect in a murder case won election into the Senate while still in prison custody for a capital crime. Many more highly placed individuals have died at the hands of bandits and criminals since then, and no one has been able to unravel the mystery behind these deaths. The story of Anambra is a particularly graphic illustration of the regime of impunity in contemporary Nigeria.

What we have actually witnessed in Nigeria in the last few years, is the failure of state and the collapse of governance. There is nothing on the ground to demonstrate that ours is not a land run over by political bandits, ethnic warlords and religious fanatics. Where one part of the country can decide to enforce criminal elements of the Islamic legal code that are clearly at variance with the nation's constitution, cutting off the limbs of petty offenders, condemning poor adulterers to death by stoning, and harassing those who do not share their faith every so often, the impression created is that no one is in charge of our affairs, and there is no law and order in place.

The average citizen now seems to have lost confidence in the capacity of those in power to protect lives and property. With a selfless, visionary and prudent leadership, the thousands of deaths we have recorded, and the millions of Naira worth of property that have been destroyed in the last few years, could have been avoided. I hold the current leadership of the Nigerian State responsible for the massive destruction of lives and property in Kaduna, Jos, Kano, Zaria, Bauchi and elsewhere, over the Sharia controversy, and at the hands of Islamic fundamentalists, because the president and his team have remained indolent and insensitive in the face of a very explosive situation.

I hold President Obasanjo and his team accountable for the blood and tears in Kaduna and other parts of the North, where non-Muslims have lost their right to live in peace, for it is the primary duty of government to protect innocent and law-abiding citizens from the nefarious activities of hooligans, bandits and fanatics. I hold those in power responsible for the pain and anguish that is the lot of the innocent citizens of Northern Nigeria who for the umpteenth time have been rendered refugees in their own country, because I expect them to own up to their ineptitude and resign from their high offices, if their being in office makes no difference for the internal security of the nation.

True, after three and a half years in government, the present crop of leaders has done little to improve the lot of Nigerians. The economy remains comatose in a country that is otherwise abundantly blessed by the Creator. Unemployment, especially youth unemployment, has soared, as a result of which the mass of our young people are losing hope and losing patience. Our schools, hospitals, and other social infrastructure are in an embarrassing state of decay. The population itself is more divided today than it ever was, since the end of 1967-1970 civil war. And now religious violence has been added to our multiple woes. Yet, in the midst of all these calamities, our leaders are carrying on business as usual.

Our public office holders are feeding fat on our scarce resources, selling the poor for a pair of sandals and playing games with the fate and fortune of our children. There are allegations and counter-allegations of bribery, running into hundreds of millions of Naira, and involving high-ranking members of the legislature and the executive. Young Nigerians have become angry, restive and violence prone. They are capitalising on anything they can find to vent their anger. Yesterday it was ethnicity. Today it is religion. Tomorrow it may be political affiliation. And there are politicians who fan these flames of violence for their own selfish political advantage. But where does all these leave Nigeria?

In the midst of the madness of today peace-seeking Nigerians and civil society groups must begin to take the elected representatives of the people to task with regard to their commitment or otherwise to creating the enabling environment for peace and social well-being. The saner elements in our society must begin to take the president, the governors, the local government chairmen and the lawmakers at all levels to task on their capacity or otherwise to formulate and defend such legal instruments and pursue such policies that will make for peace, security and prosperity.

It is not enough for us to desire peace for our land. We must be peacemakers as well. We must be committed to designing strategies to forestall, manage and resolve conflict situations. We must work hard and make sacrifices towards the attainment of the peace of our dream. The men and women of goodwill in Nigeria must constantly be on the watch to ensure that in our evolving democracy, such agents of destabilisation as the gang of Islamic fanatics in the North and their collaborators elsewhere do not hijack our commonweal for selfish political gains, and transform our land to a theatre of war, a war with no discernible reason and one without frontiers. In the midst of the madness of today those who still have their heads in place must reflect together and rise up in defence of the rule of law, or else Nigeria may soon become another Sierra Leone. A stitch in time saves nine, they say. So what do we do as elements and stakeholders in society to salvage our country from the hands of bandits and hooligans?

Chapter Twenty Two | George Ehusani

CHAPTER TWENTY THREE

Dancing on the Brink of Disaster
(An Open Letter to President Olusegun Obasanjo, May 6, 2006)

Your Excellency, at the end of their March 2006 Plenary Meeting, the Catholic Bishops of Nigeria issued a statement on the state of the nation in which they reflected on the controversial Constitutional Amendment, and particularly on the treacherous Third Term Agenda, which as at that time had already begun heating the polity very seriously. In their statement, the Bishops admitted that a review of this country's Constitution with the aim of redressing the structural injustices and shortfalls embedded in the existing one, is indeed a necessity if our fledgling democracy must survive.

With regard to the contentious proposal for a Third Term for the President and Governors, the Bishops made three clear statements: Firstly, that this issue should be a truly fair decision of Nigerians, and not the result of manipulation for self-perpetuation in office against the wish of the people; secondly, that whatever the outcome of the debate, the eventual choice of President and Governors in 2007 must be that of the people in a free and fair election; and thirdly, that even if a third term is made legal through a constitutional amendment process, those presently in power should consider whether it is ethical for them to change the rules to their advantage midway in the game. They warned that "our country cannot live in hope if government engages in a monologue, neither listening to the people nor to the international community."

Your Excellency, I have paraphrased above the position of the Catholic Bishops of Nigeria on the ongoing third term debacle. You can appreciate that while avoiding equivocation, the language of the Bishops is nevertheless diplomatic and non-confrontational as is meet for leaders in their position. But in my personal capacity as a Nigerian citizen, I have no such constraints in language or content when propelled to communicate my opinion to you and to fellow Nigerians on critical national issues. In other words, I am writing this letter to you in a frank, blunt and unequivocal manner as a significant stakeholder in the

Nigerian project, yet with due deference to your person and your revered position as President of this great country.

Events in Nigeria in the last two months (that is, since the Bishops released their communiqué) have sadly demonstrated that the "manipulation for self-perpetuation in office against the wish of the people" which the Bishops warned against is exactly what is currently playing out. From the mysterious appearances of "fake" Draft Constitutions in the 2005 National Political Reform Conference, through the dubious enterprise and show of shame which was called Zonal Public Hearings on Constitutional Amendment and the primitive rascality that enthroned a new leadership in Oyo State, to the ongoing intimidation, harassment and coercion of opponents of the Third Term Agenda, it has been a blatant display of political brigandage at the highest precincts of governance in our land.

Your Excellency, I am not only a human being, who, like other human beings have some knowledge of good and evil, I am also a Christian subscribing to a set of high moral standards as contained in Matthew chapter 5 to 7. What is more, I am a priest who has a prophetic calling to discern evil and to denounce it, in order to save the people as individuals and as a corporate entity of the unwholesome consequences of such evil. I recognize that as Scripture says, I shall be held responsible if I remain silent and refuse to speak out as I watch in broad daylight a band of misguided professional politicians and a gang of shameless sycophants daily fanning the flame of a violent revolution and stoking the embers of an inexorable disintegration.

It is for this reason, and with a high sense of responsibility that I have chosen this extraordinary medium - to address an open letter to you at this time, seeing how all other channels of alerting you on the dangers ahead (such as the Bishops' Communique referred to above) have been ignored. I am aware that similar letters have been addressed to you in the past by such eminent Nigerians as Professor Wole Soyinka, Retired Col. Abubakar Umar and of late Chief Awoniyi, but their warnings have not been heeded. Yet, I must add my voice to the other voices of reason in the land, urging you to have a rethink and see the accident ahead before it occurs.

Your Excellency, on the substantive issue of this letter, I am aware that you have not come out openly to declare your interest to contest for a third term as President in the 2007 Elections. Yet your vague and ambivalent statements when confronted on the issue in public within and outside Nigeria, your body language, and the ongoing intimidation, coercion and marginalization of all those opposed to the idea of a third term by elements associated with you and your administration - all these affirm the belief of most Nigerians today that you are poised to continue as President beyond May 2007, at whatever cost to the country, even in blood and tears. The majority of Nigerians see the failed National Confab and the ongoing charade of Constitution Amendment as part of the script for actualizing this vaunting and overarching ambition.

As a human being, I give it to you Sir, that there may be no limit to your ambition to preside over the affairs of this country, so as to consolidate the political and economic gains of your leadership as your supporters have often sought to articulate. So, you might even wish to be president for life as we have had numerous cases in Africa. Yet, it is a well-known fact of history that leaders that overstay their welcome, no matter how well they may have performed, have often been humiliated out, if they do not succeed in throwing their country into chaos. But we have gone beyond the age of Monarchies and Dynasties. We are in a democracy. Terms and term limits for public officers are fundamental to this system of government. Not only would democracy be fatally wounded if these term limits are violated or manipulated for selfish purposes, but the country itself could be turned into political turmoil as a result.

Besides, Your Excellency, the matter of a Third Term for you and others has a moral imperative. As a Christian I want you to recognize that even if through the ongoing process in the Assembly the Constitution is amended to include a third term for the President, it is immoral, unethical, and I dare say gravely sinful, for you, Chief Olusegun Obasanjo as our current (two-term) President, to seek to benefit from this term extension, because there is an elementary principle of justice and an age-old wisdom that you cannot be an umpire and a player at the same time, and that you cannot change the rules of the game midway in the game and seek to benefit from the change.

You see, as I was contemplating on this letter, I chanced on a video documentary produced by Caritas International on the protracted war in the Democratic Republic of Congo, which was caused and has been sustained all the while by the crisis of leadership in that country, including the late Mobutu Sese Sekou's ambition to remain in power for life. The level of physical devastation, the magnitude of human waste, the beastly rape of women and the hopelessness of children reflected in the documentary, present a frightening scenario that you cannot wish for this country or for any country for that matter.

Your Excellency, let me conclude my letter by reminding you of the Yoruba saying that: *"Eni ti awon orisa ba fe parun ni won n koko ya ni were"* which translates as, "the one whom the gods want to destroy, they first make mad." Therefore, I plead with you in the name of the God we both serve: **Don't do it! Stop the madness over a third term! Call to order your fanatical supporters, including those political prostitutes, contract chasers and professional sycophants who today are prodding you on in this lecherous enterprise!** And May the Good Lord bless you as you heed this humble advice in Jesus' name. Amen.

CHAPTER TWENTY FOUR

The Challenge of Leadership
(Written on October 1, 2006)

In the animal kingdom, leadership belongs to the strong and valiant, to the daring and courageous, but behind these attributes is always the need to protect the weak of the clan, to hold and defend territory, to feed and train the young and to promote discipline and well-being among the herd. In the human society the burden of leadership naturally falls upon a charismatic, selfless, and service-driven individual whose power is rooted in the transparent determination to use individual strength and wisdom, unity of purpose and the entrenchment of group order for the benefit of all.

The human being has impacted negatively or positively on this social balance by the way in which he applies his innate endowments to his environment. A wicked and roguish disposition produces despots and tyrants. A sensible, compassionate, and judicious inclination yields the charismatic type of leader and cultivates a loyal and loving following. An inept, lacklustre and passive leader erodes confidence and elicits ridicule and opprobrium. The gregarious nature of man underscores the constant interplay of human forces and interests in the unending search to fill leadership roles. Leadership is therefore not anything anyone is born with, nor anything thrust upon anyone. Authentic leadership in the human society is not anything to be obtained through conquest or by the use of all available instruments of coercion. Authentic leadership is something to merit and earn, something that carries with it certain basic qualities accruing from latent and discernible abilities.

The good leader bears an acute sense of sacrifice and always shows a bias for the care and concern of the people. The good leader has an uncanny sensitivity to people's needs and a veteran's ability to manage the people's resources. In time of crisis the good leader is an agent of reconciliation, one who shows unlimited commitment to reconciling disparate and contradictory forces. The good leader does not demand loyalty but is one whose charisma, candour and moral standing attract popular acclaim. A good leader does not predicate his reputation on propaganda nor on the patronising efforts of sycophants and hirelings.

What we have as leadership at various levels today in our society is often a pollution of the very concept of leadership and a bastardization of the values and attitudes associated with it. What we have as leadership today is often an adulteration of courage and valour and a shameful display of spineless acquiescence. What we have as leadership is often an uncharitable display of material arrogance and a distasteful reminder of group exploitation and manipulation. The bottom line for good leadership is not across the foot of the lineage ladder up the royal genealogical tree, but a transparent identification with the aspirations and expectations of the people. The bottom line for good leadership is not the guile of the mercurial politician who succeeds in hoodwinking his way to public office and proceeds methodically to strip the public treasury for his own pocket and for those of his fellow travellers.

Leadership must meet certain criteria of assessment to retain the people's popular appeal. What are the democratic principles at play, and under what form of judicial arrangement? Is there a fair and equitable distribution of wealth and resources? Are all members of the society exposed to equal opportunities? To what degree is the class system accentuated in the social structures? Are basic rights and freedoms respected and are all citizens accorded equal protection? Only when these and other positive social factors coincide in the leader of feudal stock can leadership under him be authentic. The distinction must therefore be made that a leader is a good leader not because he has feudal roots but because he possesses the tested qualities of good leadership. Society needs to continually reassess and re-evaluate qualities for leadership and demand those qualities of their potential leaders at all levels. This is the only way society can influence the type of leadership it gets and conversely, get the leadership it deserves.

In Nigeria there remains a yawning vacuum to be filled by leaders of vision and courage propelled by a single-minded determination to mobilise the people towards the achievement of the much-desired national reconciliation, social cohesion, political stability, economic prosperity and peace. We need leaders with the required wisdom and political will to champion the harnessing of the enormous natural and human resources of our land for the upliftment of all. We need leaders with a well thought out agenda for the transformation of our degenerate educational and health institutions, leaders that can restore hope to our despairing youth population whose frustrations are today manifested in widespread banditry, criminality and prodigality.

The task before the emergent leaders of our land is not a small one. The challenge before those who wish to lead Nigerians in the future is an enormous one. Thus, our long hangover in a tyrannical mind-set must quickly give way to a pluralistic and democratic society which alone will survive the challenges of the twenty-first century. Limiting leadership to campaigning for political positions and perquisites is a futile exercise in social inertia and economic stagnation. Nigeria is yearning for leaders with the necessary charism and integrity to champion the cause of channelling into productive enterprise, the many able-bodied but unemployed youths who are presently engaged in street thuggery, political banditry, drug peddling and secret cults.

Those who wish to be recognised as genuine leaders of Nigeria in Twenty-First Century must demonstrate a capability to reconcile divergent views and harmonise disparate interests in the land, since a house divided against itself cannot stand. Aspiring leaders in the Nigerian society of tomorrow must show a scorecard of performance and accountability in the services previously rendered to the people, on the local, state, or national level. Those who want to be acknowledged as leaders in our land must demonstrate their nationalism and patriotism by their self-sacrifice, their generosity, their sensitivity, and their commitment to the common good of all Nigerians.

CHAPTER TWENTY FIVE

Of Rogues, Gangsters and Politicians
(Written on May 23, 2007)

T hey have made us a laughingstock in the eyes of the civilized world, these rogues, these gangsters, these warlords in the corridors of power. They have stolen the people's mandate and aborted their collective dream of a land of peace, security and prosperity, these bandits, these criminals, these usurpers of the people's commonweal. Those the London *Economist* recently referred to as "rotten leaders," have trampled on all truth and desecrated all decency, leaving the people in shock and angry desperation. From Abia to Zamfara, and from Ekiti to Ebonyi, the evil genii have conspired to rob the people of their right to self-determination and their aspiration for self-actualisation, and sowed the seed of discord, anarchy, and doom.

The two-day war over the soul of the Nigerian nation was prosecuted on April 14 and 21, 2007. Reminiscent of the American "shock and awe" bombardment of Iraq in the year 2003, the war was prosecuted with armored personnel carriers, tanks, foot soldiers in military fatigue, combat-ready anti-riot and regular police officers, along with platoons of hired killers and dreaded thugs, menacingly brandishing loaded guns and machetes. The war was prosecuted with utmost dispatch and won by a landslide.

It is the day after this sordid victory, and as is to be expected, the scavengers are now hovering around in self-congratulatory braggadocio. As for the sycophants, the prostitutes of power and the contract chasers, they are at it again, doing what they know best. They have constituted themselves into pall bearers of a dying generation, bombarding the Newspapers and the Air waves with full page advertorials, singing the praises of our conquerors, and admonishing the "disgruntled elements" to surrender quickly so that the nation may move forward, and like the false prophets of old, they are committing the heresy of ascribing to Almighty God the messy victory of the reckless usurpers.

May 29 is the D-Day for the parade of the champions, and all is set for the shameless circus of daylight marauders that is to inaugurate yet another regime of plunder which I fear may finally nail the national coffin. And all these under the appellation of democracy. All these under the guise of government of the people, by the people, for the people. All these camouflaging as leadership, governance and politics.

This is the Nigerian brand of democracy, the jungle style survival of the fittest - a do-or-die affair. It is the resilience, or it is the recidivism of the Hobbesian primitive existence where life is "nasty, brutish and short" for the multitude of people, even in the 21st Century. It is the lot of 140 million inhabitants in a land of abundant promise whose faces are a mosaic of misery and whose bodies are a calligraphy of agony. It is the plight of over 250 ethnic nationalities otherwise generously endowed by the Creator, but now reduced to a hellhole of multiple deprivations, multiple illegalities and multiple systems-failure.

Pray, where were the sages and seers when the scoundrels and the buffoons captured and domesticated the sacred precincts of national governance? Where were the saints and scholars when the clowns and the court jesters overran the polity and laid waste our national heritage? Where were the lilies and roses when the thorns and the thistles grew, spread and dominated the national landscape? Where were the bearers of truth and justice when the agents of falsehood and deceit ascended the throne and bestrode the land, poisoning the national environment and propagating the stench of discontent? Where were the shining stars and the beacons of light as the garrison commanders and the greedy godfathers conspired to dispossess Nigeria of all her dignity and respectability? And yes, where was elegant virtue when vile vice seized the mace and legislated greed and acrimony across the nation?

Now readers, if the foregoing sounds like a dirge or a soulful lamentation, it is a reflection of how much I have suffered and agonized in recent times about the only place I call home. I have traveled quite a bit in the last few months, and so have been largely absent from Nigeria in the build-up to and the eventual staging of the coup against the collective will of the people - for that is what the outcome of the 2007 general elections amounts to. Among other places, I was in Bonn Germany, Mumbai India, Maui in the mid-Pacific State of Hawaii, and in Singapore, giving lectures and making presentations on Leadership and Integrity as well as on Global Governance and Ethical Responsibility.

In the course of my travels and my presentations, I was constantly challenged or confronted with the bundle of contradictions that is called Nigeria. And on one or two occasions my moral credentials as an ethical crusader were even called to question: Why, they said, would a Nigerian living in such a morally bankrupt society (as was seen portrayed in their recent elections), come here to teach or preach to us about good governance, leadership, integrity, ethics or responsibility? "He should be told to go back home and preach to his people, for charity begins at home!"

I was derided and lampooned for coming from a tribe of fraudsters, internet scammers, treasury looters, drug pushers and election riggers. I went around with my head bowed low, bearing the burden of our national disgrace. I felt humiliated not by the acquaintances and adversaries in Singapore or Hawaii, but by our own autochthonous conquerors whose greed for money and lust for power have pushed the country into a state of acrimonious poverty and social dislocation that have assumed the moral equivalence of war – a state of affairs where illegality is the norm, where criminality is handsomely rewarded, and where gangsters and bandits call the shots and set the tone.

Yet as a man of faith, I am convinced that our fate, the destiny of our dear nation, is not entirely in the hands of these warlords. My faith tells me that the court jesters shall not have the last laugh. I know for sure that soon, very soon, we shall be liberated from these criminals, these gangsters, these usurpers. The transformation shall come about either by design or by default, such as the aftermath of a general systems collapse that appears imminent to me. But it shall surely come about, for as presently constituted, the superstructure we have in place is only a pack of cards. It will soon come crashing down!

CHAPTER TWENTY SIX

Nigeria: Flawed Elections and the Challenge
of Nation Building
(Written on July 17, 2007)

In April 2004, the German Joint Conference Church and Development (GKKE) hosted a Workshop in Berlin with the theme: "Hot Spot Nigeria." There was high level participation from Nigeria, including members of the hierarchy of both Catholic and Protestant Churches, senior Government Officials, Civil Society Activists and Representatives of the Oil Sector. On the German side were some members of the Parliament, functionaries of the German Ministry of Development Cooperation, representatives of Political Foundations, *Misereor*, EED, and such other non-Governmental Organisations. The Workshop was aimed at not only highlighting before the German people and Government the numerous crises - Ethnic, Religious, Political, that had engulfed this most populous African nation soon after its return to democracy, following decades of military dictatorship, but also at jointly seeking possible solutions to these problems and helping Nigeria move towards a more just, peaceful and democratic nation, to the immediate benefit of Nigerians and the ultimate benefit of the global community.

Three years down the line however, and precisely June 15 to 17, 2007, the Protestant Academy in Loccum, Germany, had cause to host a similar Workshop, bringing together once again stakeholders from Nigeria and Germany to brainstorm on the Nigerian problematic. Under the rather curious theme, "Nigeria: Too Rich for Dignity and the Law?" and coming shortly after the flawed 2007 general elections in Nigeria, the Workshop was yet another occasion to focus attention on the contradictions of Nigeria and attempt to draw up recommendations on the way forward.

At the Loccum Conference, one Heinrich Bergstresser, a German participant who has spent many years researching on Nigeria, observed that Nigerians are an extremely creative and constructive people, but that there is in the country what he called *"a destructive undercurrent"* that accounts for the *fragile balance* which has been the fate of the country since its Independence from the British. What according to this speaker is missing is "some *initial spark* that would turn the fragile balance closer towards the first stage of nation building." Unfortunately, whatever this "initial spark" is has remained elusive, and in my opinion the terrible outcome of the 2007 general elections seems to have rendered the "fragile balance" even more precariously fragile.

The 2007 Elections and the events leading up to it were indeed a major national disaster, but one contrived by the ruling elite and championed by the ex-President, Olusegun Obasanjo. Nigerians had in 2006 stridently defeated Obasanjo's bid to tinker with the Constitution and go for a third term in office. The controversy or is it the turmoil generated by this singular ambition had dominated the national landscape for the better part of his second term in office, splitting the ruling party into warring factions, ridiculing the presidency, poisoning the polity and consequently heightening the tension in the land. After failing in his bid for a third term, it appeared that Obasanjo and his supporters became determined to rule Nigeria by proxy. They mobilized the immense oil resources at their disposal and utilized every means, foul and fair, to see that their own choice of candidate emerged as President, and in like manner plant their cronies into several positions in the various states. At one point Obasanjo inauspiciously declared publicly that the 2007 elections were "a *do-or-die* affair." No wonder that the General Elections were far from being peaceful, free, fair or democratic. Instead, the exercise amounted to a war against the Nigerian people. The war was prosecuted with utmost dispatch and won by a landslide, leaving the people in shock, consternation and angry desperation.

The flawed Elections of April 2007 constitute a major setback on our way to building a just, democratic and peaceful Nigeria. What Heinrich Bergstresser called "destructive undercurrents" mitigating against all progress in our otherwise abundantly endowed and potentially great country were definitely at play in the electoral exercise, as the ruling elite, whose greed for money and lust for power had earlier pushed the country into a state of acrimonious poverty and social dislocation, now presided over the installation of mediocre functionaries and charlatans at various levels, forcing Nigerians of integrity and credibility to disengage.

In a paper presented at the Loccum Workshop on Nigeria, Professor Attahiru Jega, Vice Chancellor of the Bayero University, Kano, Nigeria, described the succession of Nigerian leaders in the following words: "With very few exceptions, our crop of so-called leaders has essentially been self-serving rulers, some even despots... They lack vision, focus, selflessness and even enlightened self-interest. Most of our so-called leaders are unimaginably corrupt; they are greedy, they are vindictive, they are reckless and in many fundamental respects, senseless and even careless... There is perhaps no other country in the world where power corrupts, and absolute power corrupts as absolutely as in Nigeria."

On May 29, 2007, a new administration assumed power at both the Federal and State levels, but with a heavy burden of illegitimacy as a result of the monumental fraud that brought many of them into power. However, as the dust is settling after the installation of this new set of leaders, we observe that many principled Nigerians who cannot make sense out of the entire charade, have become cynical, apathetic, despondent and resentful.

The generality of Nigerians have become more and more distrustful of government and therefore in many areas of life they are resorting to self-help. What prevails in Nigeria today therefore is not genuine peace, but the peace of the graveyard. It is the entrenchment and consolidation of the status quo, the "fragile balance" referred to earlier, which has consistently benefited a tiny cabal, at the expense of the overwhelming majority of Nigerians who are abandoned to acrimonious poverty, insecurity and social dislocation.

The Nigerian situation is not irredeemable. Nigerians are not a different breed of human beings from citizens elsewhere such as in Singapore or Malaysia, South Africa or Ghana. Many of us do not believe that Nigeria is so difficult to organize and lead unto peaceful co-existence, political stability and economic prosperity. Yet, if this country of 140 million people must make any headway, if the progressive decay in the polity must be halted, if the descent into anarchy in Nigeria must be averted, if in the words of Heinrich Bergstresser the fragile balance must be tilted towards the first stage of nation building, then it cannot be business as usual. There must be a paradigm shift. Major far-reaching changes must take place at the level of the conduct of public officers, at the level of the people's perception of and participation in governance, and perhaps more critically, at the level of the constitutional arrangements that bind us together.

As a people, we need a new definition of leadership as service and a fresh perception of politics as the noble art of negotiating the stewardship of a society. We need to put in place new arrangements that would ensure that the paths to public service are not as smooth and attractive as they are now for rogues, thieves and brigands, and that the gains of office are not as rewarding as they are today for those who keep the keys of the national treasury. We need a shift in leadership focus in a new culture of governance, sustained by transparency and accountability, where civil society will engage the political leadership in balancing the laws of the nation and its policy objectives against concrete acts of governance.

The generality of Nigerians have an enormous task ahead. Those of us who have had to put up with a succession of rogue leaders and whose sensibilities are today continually insulted by punitive overlords in the corridors of power will not arrive at the promised land without some striving. We must wake up from our slumber and reaffirm our belief in the sovereign power of the people. The Nigerian citizenry must shake off its shackles, break out of its reactive disposition, become more proactive, engage the leadership more constructively, and begin to mould a new culture and redefine a new character of governance for the Nigerian nation, and set the agenda for its leadership.

The desired change will come about only when the various stakeholders in the Nigerian society staunchly reject the status-quo – the ignominious system that throws up for leadership positions men and women of base character and dubious wealth, whose ascension into power is often further compromised by questionable electoral credentials. The desired change will come about only when Civil Society identifies and rejects the political parasites who are isolated and alienated from the social circumstance of the people, and who do not share in the economic austerity of the moment but whose interests lie in living on a different level, thereby contributing to state failure. Those who have found their way into leadership positions today through foul and unfair means, and others who are waiting for their turn to grab the keys of the national, state or local treasury, will do well to read the signs of the times and to heed the admonition for change in leadership style and actualise such positive dreams as will pull the country from the brink.

To many observers and commentators, the Nigerian problem is as complex and multi-dimensional as its diverse peoples and cultures and religions. There appears to be too many contradictory forces at play in the Nigerian polity, hence the ethnic rivalries, the religious crises, the political logjam and the social upheaval. But for me Nigeria's ethnic, religious, cultural and political diversities do not in themselves constitute a critical setback in the process of development and democratization. Governments exist precisely to reconcile divergent views, conflicting interests and contradictory forces. In the course of history, leaders have emerged and made their marks, who, by their personal charism, their selflessness, courage and rare commitment to the common good, succeeded in building one nation and one people out of several distinct nationalities, cultures and religions.

The Nigerian problematic boils down to leadership failure. The fragile balance in which the Nigerian state presently subsists has been kept in place deliberately by those who are benefiting from the status-quo - the small tribe of autochthonous conquerors, the corrupt and punitive political elite whose members can be found in the North as well as in the South, and among Christians as well as among Muslims, in Military uniform as well as in Civilian garb. Rather than face the challenges of building a nation and making the sacrifices required to midwife one people out of the rich diversities to be found in our land, these callous rulers have all the while been gambling with the fate of 140 million people, making self-serving deals, conspiring and manipulating among themselves over the Nigerian state, and in the process squandering the resources and abandoning the people to degrading poverty.

On the other hand, an exemplary, visionary, selfless, accountable, servant leadership would succeed in mobilising the people towards the achievement of the much-desired national reconciliation, social cohesion, political stability, economic prosperity and peaceful co-existence. A determined and committed leadership, with the required wisdom and political will can champion the harnessing of the enormous natural and human resources of Nigeria for the betterment of all.

From the foregoing therefore I believe that no effort should be spared by relevant agents of Civil Society in order to meet the challenge of nurturing good leaders for the Nigerian people. The situation on the ground demands that the best of our human resources and a sizeable proportion of the financial resources of various organizations should be channeled into training for leadership at all levels and in every sphere of our national life.

Civil Society groups in Nigeria will need to build and enhance the capacity of the Nigerian people to set the agenda for the leadership, to monitor governance in general, to monitor the implementation of annual budgets in particular, and to insist on the highest standards of accountability in the management of state affairs. The task of budget monitoring is particularly critical, as Nigerian rogue leaders have constantly deployed their ill-gotten wealth for the rigging of elections in order to keep the status-quo in place.

Furthermore, our recent experience has shown that the mere hosting of periodic elections is not an indication of any progress towards a just and democratic society. Therefore, Civil Education at all levels and Democracy Monitoring as an ongoing venture should now assume greater importance and attract greater funding from within and outside the country for the periodic or ad hoc Election Monitoring exercise which often attracts a lot of interest and an appreciable amount of funding, but which only ends up unveiling the extent of rigging and other electoral malpractices but does not mitigate them.

If the Nigerian rulers are not to continue business as usual, the major stakeholders in the Nigerian society must immediately get to work and put-up strong advocacy mechanisms to push for:

(a) General Constitutional Reforms that will take care of the many loopholes identified in the 1999 Constitution, including the question of Federalism and Devolution of powers between the Centre and the constituent states, and the question of Resource generation and allocation or control.

(b) Electoral Reforms that will ensure that elections are more credible, and that Electoral Tribunals dispense speedily with cases of fraud and other irregularities before the swearing in of new leaders.

(c) Reform and Re-orientation of Security Agencies to make them more accountable to the Nigerian people, and not see themselves as only accountable to and protective of the interests of the ruling elite.

(d) Reform and Restructuring of the Independent National Electoral Commission (INEC), to make the Commission and its leadership truly independent and autonomous of the Presidency or the Executive arm of the Federal Government, in the appointment of its functionaries and the allocation of funds for its activities.

(e) Wholesale institutional reform that would transform the various institutions of state that are today weak, jaundiced, or comatose, into the strong and virile framework upon which good, democratic governance is to be built.

(f) An end to impunity, the entrenchment of the Rule of Law and the strengthening of the Judiciary.

Time is running out for the Nigerian leaders and people. With the widespread disengagement, bitterness and resentment in the land, and with the violence and hostage-taking in the Niger Delta that has overwhelmed the Security Forces, there are ominous signs in the horizon of an impending popular revolt. For indeed as presently constituted, the superstructure we have in place in Nigeria is only a pack of cards that will soon come crashing down. But if today the Nigerian people – both the leadership and the led, experience the much needed conversion and toe the line of sanity, we may yet pull back from the brink of disaster. The task ahead is enormous. Religious people must as usual, intensify their prayer for God's intervention and for the emergence of God-fearing leaders at all levels in the land. But we must do more than pray. They must become more pro-active by evolving various mechanisms for constructive engagement with leadership and governance at all levels.

CHAPTER TWENTY SEVEN

Nigeria: Missing Ingredients of Nation Building
*A lecture delivered on the occasion of the 10th Anniversary
of the Founding of the Lagos Resource Centre,
Victoria Island, Lagos, February 5, 2012*

A Brief Survey of Violent Conflicts in Nigeria

The Nigerian environment is sadly one of widespread anger and bitterness, hatred and resentment, on account of age-old ethnic antipathies, historical injustices, political isolation, ethnic marginalisation, economic disempowerment, and real or perceived religious persecution that today threaten the very foundation of our nation-state.

Violent conflicts resulting in massive loss of lives and property in Nigeria have not just begun with the deadly activities of the Boko Haram sect. They have been a regular feature of Nigerian life. From the operation *wetie* that rocked Western Nigeria in 1964, through the unfortunate civil war of 1967 to 1970, to the Niger Delta militant uprising of recent years; and from the Sharia riots of the year 2000 and 2001, through the sporadic carnage in Jos and its environs that has not abated since the year 2004, to the *Boko Haram* terrorist bombing campaigns that have brought upon us our latest national shock and shame; it has been a litany of violent conflicts that have tended to pitch the North against the South, Christians against Muslims, and the so-called Indigenes against the so-called Non-Indigenes, highlighting very graphically, the failure of the critical institutions of state and the fragile and tenuous nature of our corporate existence as a nation.

If we identify the above incidents as high-intensity internal conflicts, then there are others that will fall into the class of low-intensity conflicts, even if equally devastating of our national landscape. We have witnessed intermittent inter-ethnic and inter-clan conflicts all over the country, such as between the Tiv and the Jukun of Benue and Taraba States, the Ife and the Modakeke of Osun State, the Ijaw and the Urhobo of Delta State, the Umuleri and the Aguleri of Anambra State, the Ezillo and

Azza of Ebonyi State, the Egbura and Bassa of Nasarawa State, and that between Fulani herdsmen and local farmers across the entire stretch of the Middle Belt. We have seen sporadic violence at the hands of ethnic nationalists, such as the OPC. among the Yoruba and the Bakassi Boys and MASSOB Fighters among the Igbo. Local Government, State, and Federal elections have often seemed to some like a war to be prosecuted with machetes, machine guns, hand grenades and even homemade bombs, resulting in a flood of blood and tears. In a number of locations across the country, election days often feature soldiers in military fatigue, armoured personnel carriers and tanks and bomb detection and disposal squads on peacekeeping operations.

The High Cost of Conflict in Nigeria

On the whole, at a time when the country is not officially prosecuting a war, and when there are no natural disasters, thousands of Nigerians, including women and children, have died, others have suffered various degrees of physical injury, and property worth Billions of Naira have been destroyed. We have witnessed scores of thousands of internally displaced persons (or refugees) moving from North to South or squatting for prolonged periods in police and army barracks all over the place. Indeed many Nigerians have suffered emotional, psychological, economic and social trauma and dislocation on account of these crises, with hardly any hope of compensation from any authorities. The unfortunate impression has been left in the minds of many Nigerians that human life here is cheap, very cheap, and easily expendable. With the repeated failure of institutions of state to come to their aid when face-to-face with a violent aggressor, Nigerians have often resorted to jungle-style self-help, acquiring deadly weapons for self-defence and taking on revenge for losses suffered, and thereby aggravating the tension that already exists.

I am not aware of anyone or any group that has embarked on a comprehensive analysis of the cost of the numerous conflicts we have witnessed in our society since independence in 1960. We are not likely to ever be able to calculate in any detailed manner the cost of the many conflicts we have witnessed: from wasted lives to wasted property that could be reckoned in trillions of naira; the opportunity cost of school closures that keep the lives of young, intelligent people on hold; the incessant dislocation in family life, the destruction of social infrastructure; the loss of investment opportunities on account of widespread insecurity; the environmental degradation and the destruction of the social and moral fabric of the nation.

The Prevailing Angst in the Land

My dear friends, even as we speak here today, there is anger and resentment all over this country for real and perceived injustices that are yet to be addressed sufficiently in the structural configurations of our country. Many in the Igbo nation remain resentful of the rest of Nigeria for the injustices of the 1967 to 1970 civil war, the abandoned property imbroglio, and the alleged post-war marginalisation of Igbo people in some vital segments of the national economy and politics. Many in the Yoruba nation are angry with the rest of Nigeria for the injustices associated with the June 12 election annulment and alleged post-June 12 persecution and marginalisation of Yoruba people. Many from the collocation of small ethnic nationalities, which we call the Middle-Belt, are vexed by the appendage status accorded them in the power structures of our nation.

Many indigenes of the oil-producing Niger Delta (in spite of remedial measures in recent years and the ongoing amnesty programme), remain poised for a showdown with the rest of Nigeria because of the callous exploitation of their natural resources and the senseless devastation of their ecological environment for decades, while they were abandoned in a state of near destitution. Many among the Hausa and Fulani Muslims of the core North who desire to live under the supremacy of the Islamic Sharia are incensed that the rest of Nigeria wants to jettison what they see as their religious freedom. Ah yes, with practically every group in Nigeria, there is often bitterness and resentment over past hurts and wounds and structural injustices which have never been seriously addressed. The Oputa Panel (of 2001 and 2002) would perhaps have dealt with some of the contentious issues, if it had not ended the way it did, as an exercise in futility, with the recommendations swept under the carpet. Today across the country, there is intense anger, bitterness and resentment among the unemployed and impoverished youth population who have seen their dreams and aspirations for a meaningful life truncated and frustrated by a callous and profligate adult society.

I am convinced beyond reasonable doubt that there are fundamental ingredients for nation building that must be present in the right proportion in order for a stable, peaceful and harmonious nation to emerge or evolve from a collection of disparate ethnic groups, with distinct historical experiences, different cultural orientations, diverse political interests and multiple religious affiliations. The tragedy of Nigeria has been the preponderance of missing ingredients in the project of nation building. This reality throws wide open the floodgate of violent conflicts that appeared yesterday under the camouflage of ethnic hatred and today under the guise of religious intolerance. If this fundamental ailment is not addressed, it may yet take another form tomorrow, and all our peace building efforts may amount to simply dressing the surface wounds of a devouring cancer.

Ladies and Gentlemen, my argument here is anchored on my understanding of peace building as the set of mechanisms and activities aimed at achieving reconciliation, fostering trust, facilitating understanding, and promoting harmonious existence in a given community, following an armed conflict, or otherwise to forestall the occurrence or re-occurrence of armed conflict in a crisis-prone region. Peace building may also include conflict prevention initiatives not related to any recent conflict. Such peace building can be stimulated from outside, with foreign actors, such as the numerous United Nations' Peacekeeping Missions in Liberia, Sierra Leone, Sudan, Iraq or Afghanistan, or the modest efforts of several international agencies to promote peace in some of the violent flashpoints of our country.

Nation building, on the other hand, refers to the internal, organic (and of course dynamic) process by which a society identifies, discusses, contests, considers, and reaches consensus (or agreement) on **shared values, principles and norms**, galvanises **a sense of national cohesion**, consolidates **a national identity**, and forges **a sense of common purpose** and **a set of common goals** to which the society is oriented. It is the process of moulding diverse groups into a unified, cohesive, harmonious and stable national entity with a shared vision and a collective mission. Nation building, if it is to be successful, necessarily involves the active participation of all segments in the society, and the creative engagement of all citizens in the **constituting processes** of the emergent nation. Essential to the project of nation-building is a purposeful, visionary, courageous, self-sacrificing and therefore legitimate leadership. Such leadership assumes the role of the Architects, Engineers and Project Managers of the emergent nation.

With the above ingredients in place, anchored as it were by purposeful leadership, nation building will become the solid foundation for lasting peace, stability, prosperity and harmonious co-existence. When many of the above ingredients that are fundamental to nation building are missing, however, as appears to be our predicament in Nigeria, what we have is a free-for-all: intermittent conflicts, sporadic skirmishes, incessant strife, perennial social discord, sustained political tension, student cultism, the kidnap-and-settle syndrome, general lawlessness, and jungle-like anarchy. I must emphasise here that **strong, stable, unified nations are built fundamentally on values, and experience has shown that such values must proceed from leadership** if they are to take root in society.

Yet, what quality of values for nation building can we expect to emerge from the succession of rogue leaders, treasury looters, coup plotters, election riggers and punitive overloads that this land has endured (with only few exceptions) since independence? What quality of values for nation building can we get from the prebendal, self-serving, cash-and-carry politics that have held sway in these climes since independence and have constantly propped up a gang of self-perpetuating conquerors who have had absolutely no clue about what it takes to build a viable nation, let alone lay the foundation for a peaceful, stable and harmonious society? What quality of values for nation building can proceed from the rent seekers, contract chasers, and elite prostitutes of power who rely on corrupt godfathers, unlettered witchdoctors and village thugs to clinch power, and who change political affiliation each time they lose an election?

Nation Building Values also make for Peaceful Co-existence

Modern nations are built on identifiable shared values, norms and interests, which come to be known simply as core national values. They include patriotism (or the love of one's country to such an extent that one is ready to sacrifice one's life for it), an unwavering commitment to justice, discipline, the rule of law, equality of all persons under the law, equal opportunity for all segments in the federation, mutual respect for cultural and religious diversities among all constituting units and members, a priority of the common good over individual and group interests, protection of the weak against the possible excesses of the rich and powerful in society, and assurance of security of all persons who live and carry out legitimate trade and businesses anywhere and everywhere in the society, as well as leadership accountability. These are among the ingredients that make for true nation building, and they are consistent with the ingredients that make for peace.

True nation building is inherently an internal process, and as such, only the subjects of a nation can build a nation. They alone can have the ownership of the nation-building process. There are examples through the course of history, of leaders whose very lives symbolised and encapsulated the core national values upon which their nations were built and which to this day have continued to hold such nations together. They include George Washington (1732 – 1799), hero of the American Revolutionary war, first President of the United States of America, and champion of the most comprehensive democratic principles ever before applied in national governance. Washington is known by Americans as the "first in war, first in peace, and first in the hearts of his countrymen." We also have Giuseppe Garibaldi (1807 – 1882), hero, founder and unifier of modern Italy. There is Otto von Bismarck (1815 – 1898), hero and unifier of the German nation. There is Lee Kuan Yew (1923-), the first Singaporean Prime Minister, who saw to the transformation of his country from a resource-poor and terribly underdeveloped colonial outpost at independence in 1965 to a First World Asian Tiger by the time he left office in 1990.

Nearer home, we have Julius Nyerere (1922 – 1999), perhaps the godliest African statesman to date, who united two separate countries - Tanganyika and Zanzibar into what has come to be known as Tanzania and kept the diverse people of his otherwise resource-poor country in peace throughout his reign. He was fondly called *Mwalimu* (or Teacher) and *Baba waTaifa*, (meaning Father of the Nation). His legacy of integrity has continued to sustain Tanzania in peaceful co-existence over twenty-five years after he left office, while many other African countries have gone up in flames soon after their founding fathers left office. Finally, we have Nelson Mandela, Nobel Peace Prize winner and first President of post-apartheid (democratic) modern South Africa. He was an anti-apartheid activist who spent twenty-seven long years in prison, and upon his release, led his devastated country through a process of reconciliation and the complex negotiations leading up to the country's new democratic constitution. He stepped down after just one term as President and has remained a foremost international statesman.

Conclusion

Let me say in conclusion, that I see our inability to achieve peace as a failure of values, rather than a failure of techniques, strategies or expertise in security management. Boko Haram and similar criminal gangs have succeeded so far in their campaign to destabilise this country because ours is a corporate entity that is not solidly founded on those critical building blocks upon which more successful modern nations stand. I am convinced beyond reasonable doubt that our country has been in the past so prone to conflict and is today in such crisis, as a result of the fragility of its very foundations. Some have referred to the problem as fundamental flaws in the structural configuration of our country. In the foregoing presentation, I have identified it as the "missing ingredients in our nation-building project." These missing ingredients are values, principles and norms that are critical to nation building. They include patriotism, commitment to justice, human dignity and equality, discipline, the rule of law, common good imperative, mutual respect for cultural and religious diversities, equal opportunities and access to the resources of the land. To anchor these values and entrench them in the very structures of society, we require a crop of purposeful, visionary, self-sacrificing and accountable leaders, whose very lives are an embodiment of such core national values and whose disciplined conduct in public and in private affairs, are an exercise in mentoring and an inspiration to future generations of their countrymen and women.

These value-based ingredients have unfortunately been in very short supply, if not entirely missing from our national landscape, and we as a people have continued to pay lip service to the project of nation building. But there are no short-cuts to nation building and peaceful co-existence. Nigerians desirous of peace and stability in this polity must invest today in what has been established as the critical building blocks of a modern nation-state, if we are ever going to have a viable nation with sustainable peace. While the security agencies grapple with the technicalities of fighting such criminal gangs as Boko Haram, the rest of us must invest heavily in leadership training and in the dissemination of the nation-building values outlined above.

We must each take an interest in politics and in the quality of persons that assume public office. We must take responsibility for the future and do all we can to stop the thugs and the rogues, the charlatans and mediocre performers who now populate the corridors of power and who are bent on ruining this nation. Until now, it has been garbage in, garbage out, but the ugly trend can and must be reversed. So let those among us who have any serious commitment to the survival of our corporate entity invest some time and resources in promoting what we have identified as the value-based ingredients of nation building, towards the emergence of a viable nation of sustainable peace, harmonious existence and economic prosperity.

CHAPTER TWENTY EIGHT

Elite Conspiracy in the Nigerian Ruination
*(Paper presented at the 5th Town Hall Meeting of the Strategic
Assembly for Leadership Thrust, Abuja, June 26, 2016)*

The Nigerian nation is today hanging peremptorily at the edge of a precipice, on account of the fundamentalist Islamic insurgency in the Northeast, the resource control militancy in the South-South, the Biafran ethnic irredentist crusade in the Southeast and the intermittent rumbles of the Oodua Peoples Congress in the South-West. Sandwiched between these high-intensity expressions of group discontent in the North, South, East and West, are the flashpoints of ethno-religious violence and the so-called herdsmen versus local farmers conflicts that have gone on for decades in most of the Middle Belt States, and only now have gained national and international attention after a recent incursion of the herdsmen into farming communities in Ondo, Enugu, Abia and Bayelsa States.

Violent conflicts resulting in massive loss of lives and property in Nigeria have not just begun with the deadly activities of the latter-day insurgents in the North and in the South. Violent conflicts have been a regular feature of Nigerian life since independence. From the operation *wetie* that rocked Western Nigeria in 1964, through the unfortunate civil war of 1967 to 1970, to the Niger Delta militant uprising of the last decade; and from the Maitatsine uprising of 1982, through the sharia riots of year 2000 and 2001, to the sporadic carnage in Plateau, Taraba, Kaduna, Bauchi, and Nasarawa States, as well as the intermittent fratricidal and clannish conflicts in Osun, Anambra, Ebonyi, Delta, Rivers and Bayelsa States, it has been a litany of violent conflicts that have tended to pitch the North against the South, Christians against Muslims, and the so-called Indigenes against the so-called Non-Indigenes, highlighting very graphically the tenuous nature of our corporate existence, the abysmal failure of the critical institutions of state and the absence from our public space of the fundamental values that would have transformed us into a stable, peaceful, and prosperous nation.

As we are polarised and prone to conflict along ethnic and religious lines, so are we polarised and prone to conflict along political lines, even when the political parties are largely devoid of ideological content. Rather than seeing it as a game of compromise and healthy competition for public office, Nigerians have been approaching politics with a killer's touch, using all manner of deadly manoeuvres to gore at political adversaries. Local Government, State and Federal elections have often seemed to some like a war to be prosecuted with machetes, machine guns, hand grenades and even home-made bombs, resulting in a flood of blood and a stream of tears. In a number of locations across the country, election days often feature soldiers in military fatigue, armoured personnel carriers and tanks, as well as bomb detection and disposal squads on peacekeeping operations. It has indeed been politics of acrimony, where the public space is dominated, not by elite debate over alternative approaches to issues of national development, but where age-old ethnic antipathies and acrimonies are often resurrected and played out in the most shameless and reckless manner for selfish advantage.

This is not a feature to be found only among old-breed politicians. Today's social media, dominated as it is by young, educated people, far from being a space for civilised discourse, is often awash with insults, abuses, curses, and the exchange of acrimonious and slanderous posts. Young people from across the geographical and ethnic divide, who attended the same secondary schools and universities, who do business together, who share office space and who sit side by side in church, turn out to be vicious warriors on Facebook or Twitter – simply on account of the ethnic identity of their parents, or their real or perceived political leanings. The social media is being used by many reckless and unscrupulous bloggers to promote hatred and (with the possibility of photo-shop and cleverly doctored video clips), they broadcast such outright falsehood that is capable of inciting an already bitterly divided population to war.

Commenting on the senselessly polarised reaction of Nigerians to the ongoing mind-boggling revelations of the colossal sums looted from government treasury by some functionaries of the last administration and their cronies, Social Commentator and Human Rights Lawyer Festus Keyamo says in a recent post: *'One can constructively criticise a government on different issues, but to oppose a government for recovering monies belonging to all of us, I don't get it. I thought that on the aggressive recovery of loot, partisanship would be put aside, and everyone would come together and say thank you to the Federal Government."* He makes this analogy: *"An armed robber robs a neighbourhood. A man pursues him and recovers the loot. You come out and you fume at the man for tackling the robber too hard."* He concluded the post by saying: *"This is insanity."*

My dear friends, as the Nigerian elite from North to South and from East to West conduct their lives or carry out their business each day, they harbour intense, pent-up anger and resentment for real and perceived injustices that they have failed to address sufficiently in the structural configurations of the country. Many in the Igbo nation remain resentful towards the rest of Nigeria for the real and perceived injustices of the 1967 to 1970 civil war, and the alleged post-war marginalisation of Igbo people in some vital segments of the national economy and politics. Many in the Yoruba nation are angry with the rest of Nigeria for the injustices associated with the June 12 election annulment, and the alleged post-June 12 persecution and marginalisation of Yoruba people. Many from the collocation of small ethnic nationalities which we call the Middle Belt, are vexed by the appendage status accorded them in the power structures of our nation.

Many indigenes of the oil producing Niger Delta (in spite of the Amnesty Programme of the Yar'adua and Jonathan regimes), remain poised for a showdown with the rest of Nigeria, because of the callous exploitation of their natural resources and the senseless devastation of their ecological environment for decades, while they were abandoned to a state of near destitution. Many among the Hausa and Fulani Muslims of the core North who desire to live under the supremacy of the Islamic Sharia are incensed that the rest of Nigeria wants to jettison what they see as their religious freedom. Ah yes, with practically every group in Nigeria, there is often bitterness and resentment over past hurts and wounds and structural injustices which have never been seriously addressed, in spite of the many national conferences held in the past. So we visit our anger on one another at the slightest provocation, abusing and cursing, killing and maiming, and burning down whole towns and villages.

The moral fabric in Nigeria has suffered a fatal assault. We are today confronted with the reality of a naked public square in our national life, whereby top level retired and serving Government Officials, including State Governors and Ministers of the Federal Republic, Legislators, Legal Luminaries and Jurists, Army Generals, Business Executives, Chiefs and even Religious Leaders, are daily paraded in court, accused of stealing humongous sums of money from the public treasury. Today's generation of Nigerians appear in large measure to have lost the sense of right and wrong, of values and vices, of what is desirable and what is condemnable, of what is good and what is bad. This is why when our tribesman or woman is accused of stealing four billion naira that was meant for fighting Boko Haram insurgency or embezzling two billion naira intended for the purchase of critical hospital equipment in the state, we come out in our thousands, carrying placards to protest what we call a lopsided fight against corruption, and threatening to burn down the country if the authorities do not leave our tribesman alone!

True, as a corporate entity we seem to have lost quite a dose of our sense of shame and outrage at the preponderance of corruption and the reign of impunity. We carry on our criminal exploitation of a dysfunctional and disdainful social system as if indeed we dwell in a jungle where might is right, and where the gangsters and the fraudsters are the heroes and heroines that are constantly being rewarded and decorated with national honours, chieftaincy titles and plum political appointments.

Proverbs 29:18 says where there is no vision, the people perish. In Matthew 6:22 Jesus says "The eye is the lamp of the body. If your eye is sound, your whole body will be full of light; but if your eye is unhealthy, our whole body will be full of darkness. If then the light in you is darkness, how great is the darkness. The scandal of contemporary Nigeria is, in my view, the ascendancy of elite debauchery and the preponderance of the cult of mediocrity in practically all spheres of our national life. Whereas Nigerians brandish more impressive academic credentials than perhaps citizens of any other African nation, and whereas Universities and other tertiary institutions are littered all over the place, Nigeria today perishes for lack of knowledge. As a people we groan under the weight of our collective myopia. There is an acute shortage of vision, intellectual rigour and critical thinking even in academic circles. What appears to be in place is the cult of mediocrity, whereby professors of political science who teach the value and principles of democracy, and have written volumes of books on good governance, legal luminaries who hold the title of "Senior Advocate of Nigeria," and who have sworn to defend the rule of law, and highly respected religious prelates, who are expected to hold truth as sacred, now dance naked in the public square, revelling in falsehood, carrying on a lifestyle of primitive accumulation, commanding the brigade of ethnic bigotry, promoting a culture of impunity in the land.

A few years ago, I wrote the following poem which I titled "**Scandal**." It goes thus:

Daddy has eaten the sour grapes
And today my brothers and sisters
Are gnashing their teeth
Mommy has tasted the forbidden fruit
And now the kids are out
Naked in the cold

They have desecrated the tree of love
And violated the sanctuary of justice
And so the children flee from wisdom's child
And fall into the callous embrace
Of the angel of death

Tomorrow has become a stone wall
That my brothers and sisters stare at
With angry desperation

Cursed be that blind day
When daddy resolved to steal food
Off the hands of his own children
Alas for that dark hour
When mummy chose to mortgage tomorrow
For the fleeting pleasures of today.

(From *Petals of Truth* by Fr. George Ehusani, 1998, page 105).

There is this Greek saying that *"A society grows great when leaders plant trees under whose shade they know they will never sit."* Great societies are built by leaders who plant Oak trees, Iroko trees and Baobab trees. These trees take hundreds of years to mature. Afterwards they are the sturdiest and strongest trees in the forest. But what kind of trees do our own leaders plant? Here in Nigeria our leaders plant pawpaw trees and pulpwood that they can harvest in two or three years. Leaders in Nigeria are often not planning for the next 25 or 50 years. They are planning for the next election exercise, simple!

We have often written and spoken of the failure of leadership in these climes. For the purpose of this discussion, we can substitute *elite class* for leadership. By elite class I mean the privileged group of Nigerians who went to school, who had a good education in Nigeria or abroad, and who are lucky to be gainfully engaged in some business or career. The elite class for me includes those whose parents went to school, who wore shoes to school, who grew up in GRAs or in some posh part of town, or those who were raised in remote villages and urban slums, but who are now privileged dwellers in the parts of our segregated cities meant for the rich only. Yes, by elite class I mean to include those who are able to ride their own cars, those who are able to build their own houses, or who can afford to live in expensive estates located in the polished segments of Abuja and other cities across Nigeria. So, the elite class in my view includes practically every one of us here today!

Ours is a tale of two cities – that of the elite (oppressor) class and that of the common (oppressed) class. The Nigerian elite class must assume a major responsibility for the mess of the moment, because, as we read in Luke 12:48, "from him to whom much has been given, much is expected." Many will agree with me that the Nigerian social dynamics have always been unjustly skewed in favour of the political, economic, religious and social elite. The Nigerian social dynamics are simply a continuation of colonial structures of oppression and exploitation, which are expressed in the following areas among others:

1. A segregated urban housing system and the emergence of slum settlements around our cities.
2. With no decent urban transportation system in place, the rich ride expensive cars and SUVs, while the poor are condemned to some rickety contraptions that serve as means of public transportation.
3. Unjust Educational System whereby practically everyone that belong to the elite class sends his or her children to expensive private

schools from monies often earned or stolen from public coffers, while public schools have been completely destroyed.

4. Unjust Health care system whereby the elite can pay for their own health care in private hospitals at home and abroad, while public health infrastructures have been neglected or are non-existent.

5. Unjust Valuation of Manual Labour whereby white-collar jobs are often rewarded 10 to 100 times over labour-intensive non-white-collar work including petty farming, domestic work, masonry, plumbing, auto mechanic, welding, etc.

6. Unfair administration of the criminal justice system whereby poor people who are apprehended for criminal offences often suffer the full brunt of the law, whereas rich suspects can afford the most qualified lawyers in the land, and thereby escape or delay justice endlessly.

Indeed, those who belong to the Nigerian elite as outlined above, do not recognise the above quoted biblical truth that "from him to whom much has been given, much is expected." Many Nigerians who today own property in the UK and the US, and those who own property and businesses in Lagos, Abuja, Port Harcourt, Enugu, Ibadan and Warri, are those who themselves or their parents benefitted from Federal or State governments scholarships to study oversees or in one of our first-generation universities. Many of them attended Unity Schools which were generously funded by government from the resources of the land. Many of them were sponsored to other Secondary Schools, Universities and Military Academies (wholly or at least in part) with public funds, and upon completion of their studies, they had jobs waiting for them, car loans were made available for them, and they replaced the white man in GRAs or V.I.P quarters.

Unfortunately, these privileged Nigerians simply took over from the colonial masters and became even more ruthless oppressors and exploiters of their own people than the colonial masters. They made no provision for decent public transportation, no provision for decent housing or functional health care facilities. They did not develop the Nigerian natural tourist attractions or build any holiday resorts in their towns and villages. Instead, they cultivated the very expensive habit of going oversees for holidays every year with their families. They did not initiate the development and processing of the numerous minerals and agricultural products of our land for construction and for food and drink. Instead, they cultivated a taste for building materials from Turkey, household furniture from Italy, expensive cars from Germany, polished rice from Thailand, fermented cheese from Holland and Royal Champagne from France.

The elite class has also often instigated violent crisis for their selfish political and economic gains: Whereas as is widely acknowledged, the ordinary man on the street and the ordinary woman in the marketplace often get along very well, living in crowded *face-me-I-face-you* homes, jointly using kitchens and bathrooms, exchanging household utensils, and setting their wares side by side in the marketplace, it is the political elite, who often, for their own selfish reasons do make these poor people begin to see their neighbours as enemies, because of where their ancestors come from.

The political elite have often set up private armies that metamorphosed into militancy and insurgency groups like Boko Haram, MEND, OPC. It is alleged that those who have turned themselves into kidnappers were once political thugs for well-known politicians. The traditional rulers and factional leaders of the Niger Delta have often become stupendously rich on account of being constantly appeased by Oil Companies or "settled" by federal government agencies, while completely neglecting the people they claim to represent. They now fly around in private jets, buy properties in Dubai, and abandon their kith and kin to destitution.

Many of those whom Nigerians identify as powerful "Men of God" are perhaps even worse exploiters of the people. While the economic fortunes and social indices of the ever gullible and vulnerable poor miracle seekers keep worsening, the private estates and empires of our celebrity men of God keep expanding. Rather than go to the urban slums and villages to set up schools and medical clinics, vocational centres and handicapped people's homes, in order to exemplify Jesus' preferential option for the poorest and the weakest of society, these "men of God" often operate only among the elite class and live scandalously rich lives funded with money raised from poor miracle seekers or otherwise from big time corrupt worshippers.

There are segments of the Nigerian elite who would like to blame all the Nigerian problem on the political stranglehold or hegemonic conspiracy of past and present functionaries from some particular ethnic groups. While this may be a convenient script so that many of us will evade responsibility for the mess we have jointly made of Nigeria, I often like to ask Nigerians: "From which part of the country is the Chairman of your local government area?" "From which part of the country is the governor of your state? From which part of the country did the legislators in your state assembly emerge?" If these are not doing well, then we must concede that our oppressors are our own kith and kin!

Perhaps the greatest failure of the Nigerian poor is their criminal acquiescence in the face of this grand conspiracy of the callous elite class to betray, exploit, oppress and subjugate them. Perhaps the greatest failure of the Nigerian masses is their refusal to rise up in revolt and say "enough is enough" to the merciless locusts that have repeatedly invaded their land, devouring their dreams and dashing their hopes of wholesome existence. Perhaps the greatest failure of the Nigerian victims of elite debauchery is their inability to forge a common perception of the challenge that faces them, and to unite or join forces to dislodge those who have stolen their present and mortgaged their future. Perhaps the greatest failure of the abused and oppressed poor across the country is that they have constantly succumbed to the false propaganda of ethnic chauvinists and the mendacious campaign of the religious bigots in our land. Yes, perhaps the greatest failure of the Nigerian poor is that they have constantly embraced the lie that those responsible for their problems are not their own brothers and sisters; that those responsible for their problems belong to the other ethnic group or the other religion; that if only one of their own could be the governor or the president; if only they could have their own local government, their own state or their own country, then they shall be happy ever after!

CHAPTER TWENTY NINE

National Unity and the Application
of the Federal Character Principle
(Written on September 18, 2017)

The unity of the Nigerian state is once again seriously compromised by deep cleavages that appear along religious and ethnic and. Beside the mega challenge of terrorist insurgency in the north, secessionist agitations in the east and the restructuring campaign everywhere else, there is today a widespread discontent over the application of the Federal Character Principle which entered the Nigerian legal and political lexicon in 1979 and is enshrined in the 1999 Constitution. The rationale for the Principle as contained in the Constitution is as follows:

> ...the government of the Federation or any of its agencies and the conduct of its affairs shall be carried out in such a manner as to reflect the federal character of Nigeria and the need to promote national unity and also to command national loyalty, thereby ensuring that there shall be no predominance of persons from a few states or from a few ethnic or other sectional groups in that government or in any of its agencies (See Section 14 (3-4) and Third Schedule, Part 1(c) of the Constitution).

The Federal Character Principle was designed to address seriously the fears of marginalization in certain sections of the country, to promote national integration and enhance unity among a people of diverse ethnic, linguistic, religious and geographical background. The desire was to unite the Nigerian people who at independence and at the time of the introduction of the principle, were at various levels of development, and very significantly at various stages of advancement in Western education. A Federal Character Commission was established via decree 34 of 1996 to drive the implementation of the Federal Character Principle. Its responsibility was "to promote, monitor and enforce compliance with the principles of the proportional sharing of all bureaucratic, economic, media and political posts at all levels of government."

Thus, the architects of the Federal Character Principle wanted to ensure that the public service and public institutions reflect the federal character of our nation, so that every constituent part of the nation is guaranteed a say and a place in the political, administrative and economic management of the federation, and in the equitable allocation of the values and benefits of our country. The principle was seen as Nigeria's path to achieving representative bureaucracy and some measure of balance among diverse ethnicities in the Federation. There was the assumption that if the public service and public corporations are truly representative, this will promote a sense of national belonging and inclusion and invariably the loyalty of everyone and the unity of the country.

Serious questions have however been raised over the manner in which the Federal Character Principle and the accompanying quota system has over the years been applied. Some critics believe that the principle has been so thoroughly exploited, so thoroughly abused and so thoroughly manipulated for selfish sectional interests, that it now fuels corruption and promotes mediocrity in every sector of the Nigerian public service, in addition to lowering the standard of education and making the pursuit of excellence in any department of our national life an unattainable ideal. Many are of the opinion that the Federal Character Principle as applied today circumvents merit and promotes unethical practices in the critical area of manpower procurement and promotion, and thus is responsible in good measure for our national underdevelopment, our fallen educational standards, our decayed social infrastructures, the poor quality of persons in political leadership, as well as our worsening security situation.

Many Nigerians are of the opinion that as applied today in the three tiers of government, as well as in admissions to educational institutions, in appointments and promotions to positions of responsibility in public service and in the siting of government institutions, the Federal Character principle rather than be a catalyst for the desired national integration, is now a reason for widespread anger and discontent, aside from being the bedrock of the gross inefficiency that today defines state bureaucracy at all levels.

A merit-based system is crucial to effectiveness and efficiency in public service delivery. The quality of human resource in any organization determines to a very high degree the quality of its outputs.

That is why organisations desiring to succeed often go head-hunting for the best and the brightest, and they promote their staff members to higher positions of responsibility, not by quota system, but by the demonstrable ability of the staff to advance the goals and objectives of the organisation. If however the public service in Nigeria can be taken as an organisation, the persons who lead or manage it have often not been the best and the brightest that the country could have. Much of this failure has been blamed on the skewed manner in which the Federal Character principle has been applied.

Nigeria is truly a multi-ethnic, multi-cultural and multi-religious society. While we must always recognize and respect the diversity of our nation, and while every part of the country must be given a sense of belonging, the application of the Federal Character principle in the processes of job recruitments and promotions, as well as admission into government-owned educational institutions has often amounted to sacrificing excellence on the altar of inclusiveness. A situation where even for positions of critical responsibility such as Departmental Directors and Permanent Secretaries of Federal Ministries, and the headship of educational and health institutions, qualified and capable persons are discarded in favour of those who are appointed simply to fill the quota of their constituencies, is nothing but the triumph of mediocrity.

This is a grave injustice not only to the more qualified individuals who have been denied positions for which they are very well qualified, but also an injustice to the entire state which, by this awkward practice, is now and again deprived of the services of competent professionals and efficient bureaucrats. Too often in our recent history, individuals and groups have used the Federal Character principle as camouflage for the placement of unqualified and incompetent cronies and kinsmen into positions of responsibility in the public service and in educational institutions. This practice which is increasingly widespread in our society has resulted in gross inefficiency, huge financial losses, widespread infrastructural decay, and the gradual ruination of public institutions.

Yet do standards really need to be lowered in order that our public service and public institutions reflect the Federal Character? No. There must be better ways of acknowledging our diversity as a nation and giving everyone a sense of belonging. To admit candidates into educational institutions, there must be certain benchmarks, below which an institution desiring excellence should not descend. When following the 2017 Joint Admissions and Matriculations Board (JAMB) exercise, the body announced the cumulative score of 120 as its minimum cut off mark for university admission, there was a major uproar across the country. Many enlightened Nigerians expressed the view that 120 out of 400 should never be considered a pass mark. And of course, a number of respectable universities immediately distanced themselves from such an abysmally low cut-off mark and insisted that they would not let anyone with that kind of score step into the grounds of their university for any course whatsoever.

How is a university expected to manage the situation whereby there are two candidates for the same course – one scoring 280 and the other scoring 120? More distressing is the scenario whereby a candidate from what is considered "educationally advantaged state" may have as high a score as 240, and will not be admitted for a particular course, whereas for the same course another candidate from what is considered "educationally disadvantaged state" is admitted with as low a score as 180. And to make matters worse, the two candidates could have had their secondary education in the same school, located in the same state, and sat for their JAMB examination at the same Centre, but their ancestors happen to have been traced to different parts of the country, identified as either educationally advantaged or educationally disadvantaged. The reaction of many young people to this kind of blatantly skewed and unjust system is anger, bitterness and resentment. And yet the scenario is played out every day with regard to admissions to government educational institutions and promotion to senior level positions in the public service. It is an uphill task to raise patriotic citizens out of young people who have experienced such structural injustices early in their formative years.

To bring up children from so-called educationally disadvantaged regions to eventually take positions in the civil service and be able to compete with their peers from the so-called educationally advantaged regions, some more creative homework has to be done. It is not the standard of education that should be lowered. A lot more commitment has to be shown by those charged with the responsibility of governance at local, state and national levels. A lot more financial investment must be made to adequately boost elementary education in those places; a lot more teachers must be trained and encouraged to give their best for the children of those places; more extra coaching of children could be done during the school term and during the holidays in those places. Perhaps the number of years for primary and secondary education in those "educationally disadvantaged" regions could be extended, so the children have more time to "catch up" with the children of the "educationally advantaged regions." In this way academic institutions are able to keep their minimum standards for admission, and every child that is admitted to any particular academic institution truly merits to be so admitted, and not just filling his or her state's quota.

The above steps should be considered along with the whole question of citizenship versus the national question, which has largely remained unresolved in our society. For selfish political reasons our leaders have consistently distanced themselves from any serious debate with regard to what really constitutes Nigerian citizenship as distinct from what we know as *"indigeneship."* Is an Igbo-speaking Nigerian who was born and raised in Kano a citizen of Kano without recourse to the so-called hometown of his ancestors? Is a Hausa-speaking Nigerian who was born and raised in Ibadan a citizen of Ibadan without recourse to whichever part of the country his ancestors are said to be from?

We are all aware that in modern societies, citizenship is first and foremost defined by place of birth. We know of many of our kith and kin who were born in the United Kingdom or the United States and are as a result automatically citizens of those countries, carrying the passports of those countries, and are able to stand for election as mayors and parliamentarians in those countries. We know that Barack Obama has a Kenyan father. But that did not stop him becoming the President of the United States of America. Our own constitution indeed provides that all children born in Nigeria are by birth automatically Nigerians. Yet we have the ugly and vexing situation whereby a child born and raised in a particular town in Nigeria for example, when seeking admission into a federal or state tertiary institution, is often required to travel to his or her ancestral homeland across the country to obtain a "citizenship certificate" that attests to the fact that the ancestors are indeed from the Local Government Area in question.

Henceforth it is this "citizenship" or more appropriately *"indigeneship certificate"* that is used to classify the child as from "educationally advantaged" or "educationally disadvantaged" area, with all the rights and privileges attached to that appellation in admission considerations.

This happens even though the child possesses a valid "birth certificate" issued by the Local Government Council of the parents' residence or where the child was born, and where the family has continued to reside. The scenario is also played out with regards to employment opportunities and promotion to senior level positions in government institutions. If this same person aspires for a career in politics, he or she may have to relocate to his or her ancestral homeland to pursue such ambition, as there is little chance of the person being nominated by any party as a candidate for election – being as such a person is called, a "non-indigene."

How could two children who were born in the same town, who attended the same elementary and secondary school, whose parents work in the same office, who live in the same estate, be treated so differently in admission requirements to higher institutions, in employment opportunities, in promotion to positions of responsibility and in prospects for career in politics? How could a society where people are daily subjected to such injustice ever hope to become united, stable, peaceful and prosperous?

The Catholic Church has done well to promote and popularize the dictum: "if you want peace, work for justice." The application of the Federal Character principle in our nation's constitution, originally intended to foster greater national integration, is now being used as an instrument of inequality and discrimination. It has become an agent of disaffection – fueling widespread anger and resentment across the land. The Federal Character principle as operative cannot enhance any measure of national integration. Rather, its application in many instances has often meant the banishment of excellence and the enthronement of mediocrity in the land, with all the consequences that follow.

If the cause of justice is to be served and our institutions are to become centres of excellence in education and service provision, then minimum standards must also be maintained in the recruitment and promotion of staff for government-owned institutions. The first stage in the recruitment process is that qualified persons from across the country are shortlisted, using the benchmark already set for the attainment of excellence. The Federal Character principle and the quota system could then be applied to select successful candidates from among the pool of highly qualified persons only. Just as no one who does not meet the minimum standards should be employed in any government institution, it is also undesirable that any staff should be promoted beyond his or her level of competence.

It is ironic that today many Nigerians feel more marginalized than was the case before 1979 and 1999. Perhaps if there was no Federal Character law, the situation could even have been worse. Poorly implemented as it may have been, it is still a major restraining force against the tendency of the average Nigerian leader to reduce everything to his or her own narrow parochial interests. Perhaps it is better to have a structure that compels functionaries of state to be inclusive in staff appointment and in the siting of institutions than to have a system where nepotism, favoritism and ethnic bigotry predominate. The first instinct of many leaders in Nigeria is often to use public funds to set up infrastructure in their own states and villages, before they think of other Nigerians. From the village and the state, they may then think of their region. The contractors are often either their friends or agents. This is the case because many Nigerians see public service as an opportunity to serve and please their own people, and not the generality of Nigerians.

In the midst of this undesirable situation, religious people have often not used religion to help sanitize society and ensure equity and justice. Some Nigerian heads of government departments have been so unscrupulous that they would insist on surrounding themselves only with their Church members or adherents of their faith. The result is a base system that stands in the way of performance and efficiency. Many have argued that the existence of a Federal Character principle is the only reason why some people still manage to pretend to be Nigerian. Without it, there would have been no way to remind people that this country cannot be run at the level of a village meeting and that it belongs to over 350 nationalities. Yet, greater emphasis should be placed on merits and standards. To rise gradually above the present mess, we must grow an enlightened society. We must foster a sense of national cohesion. We must build a nation where people are given opportunities, and are promoted, not on the basis of tribal or religious affiliations, but on the basis of their ability and the content of their character.

And to conclude this brief reflection, we must admit unfortunately that with regard to the widespread ethnic bigotry in our society, elements of the Christian Church and the Catholic Church in particular have often missed the chance to make a difference. We have often missed the chance to rise above our own entrenched parochial interests and show the light to a people groping in the dark. With our own "son of the soil" syndrome, and the scandalous controversies over appointment of bishops as well as appointments into provincial or national offices in our Church, we are hardly qualified to pontificate over this vexing problem in our society. Yet we must make a renewed commitment to truth, to justice and to the universal brotherhood of all. Beginning from our own ecclesial circles or ecclesiastical appointments, we must begin to promote a vision of society beyond our primitive ethnic limitations. We must begin to embrace goodness in people of other ethnic groups and other religions. We must begin to recognize the image of God in all human beings and acknowledge excellence wherever it is to be found. This is one way of being salt of the earth and light of the world to our people, for where there is no vision, the people perish!

CHAPTER THIRTY

Booming Religiosity and Rampant Corruption in Nigeria: Our Moral Conundrum

(A paper presented at the Conference of the Association of Local Governments of Nigeria in Abuja, November 9, 2017).

Nigerian Religiosity and the Corruption Conundrum

With all the show of religiosity or outward display of piety in Nigeria, one would have expected to see a very high degree of social morality in the country, since all world religions generally promote truth, justice, honesty and probity. But this is not to be the case with us. There is an embarrassing contradiction between the high ethical demands of the two religions which the majority of Nigerians profess, and the phenomenon of corruption, greed and graft that has earned our country an unenviable place among the gang of corrupt nations. Recall the rather unguarded but embarrassingly damning statement of the former British Prime Minister David Cameron to the effect that Nigeria and Afghanistan are the world's most fantastically corrupt countries.

While such damning verdict of a Western leader or that of Transparency International may be contested on many grounds by patriotic Nigerians, we cannot run away from the truth that in recent times corruption has almost attained the status of state policy in Nigeria. Yes, some keen observers of the phenomenon actually say that corruption is so endemic in the Nigerian society that the socio-economic and political system can almost not function without it. Corruption in its many shapes and sizes has continued to flourish in Nigeria - from the petty bribery taken by the clerk in the office or the policeman at the checkpoint, to the grand corruption by which huge project contracts are hurriedly awarded, not for the sake of the common good, but because of the greed of the awarding official, who requires some money via contract "kick-backs."

Fraud, thievery, and roguery have been the order of the day, even as our environment is awash with prayers and ritual sacrifices to the God of truth, justice and righteousness. It doesn't seem to be a matter of contradiction for many highly placed Nigerians that they embezzle or misappropriate stupendous amounts of public and company (or even church) funds, while at the same time struggling to occupy the front seats or even take religious titles and other honours in their churches and mosques. Examination malpractice is witnessed on a wide scale from the common entrance examination organised for the placement of 10-year-olds into colleges to the final qualifying examination at the Nigerian Law School. It is alleged that unscrupulous parents are not only accomplices, but sometimes initiators of these shameful practices.

Many Nigerians often fraudulently procure medical certificates of fitness from hospitals when they have not undergone any medical tests. They also obtain sick leave permits from doctors when they are hale and hearty. They sometimes falsify the age of their children and obtain fake birth certificates in order to get them into nursery or primary schools earlier than the stipulated age. Holding the Bible or Quran in court, they vow to tell the truth and nothing but the truth, only to tell a bundle of lies. They routinely swear to false affidavits in order to claim some undeserved benefits and make false age declarations when seeking employment or admission into institutions of learning. Many of those who today hold drivers' licences, have never seen what a V.I.O. or FRSC testing ground looks like. They simply pay for the licence and declare themselves drivers, putting at risk not only their own lives, but also the lives of other road users.

Many Nigerians, including seemingly pious Christians and Muslims, who would go to war in defence of their religions, have no qualms of conscience when they pay to obtain yellow cards without the necessary inoculation for which the card is supposed to be evidence. Many of our countrymen and women who flock to churches on Sunday and fill the mosques on Friday are at one time or the other involved in such fraudulent activities as evading tax, issuing and obtaining of fake receipts, over-invoicing and under-invoicing, importation of fake drugs, petty and large-scale bribery, fake audit reports, "creative book-keeping," "round-tripping," advance fee fraud, etc. All these practices are so commonplace and so widespread that many young Nigerians are today unable to distinguish between good and evil or between right and wrong.

The Local Government System and Corruption

The local government system as presently operated in many states of Nigeria is itself a metaphor for corruption, and a blatant display of impunity, with grave consequences for the overwhelming majority of Nigerians who ordinarily should expect the provision of basic health, educational and social infrastructure from the Local Government Area Councils. Whereas section 7 of the Constitution of the Federal Republic of Nigeria provides for democratically elected Chairmen and Councillors in our 774 Local Government Area Councils, we all know that in majority of our states local government chairmen and councillors are simply handpicked by the state governors, and they operate simply at the bidding and behest of the governors. What is more, the system known as "joint account of state and local governments," whereby state ministries of local governments collect federal allocations meant for local governments and in many cases remit to these statutory beneficiaries only a fraction of what is due them each month - on account of which the local government councils are rendered impotent, unable to render basic services to the people, is in large measure a monument of corruption and a grave infraction of the Constitution.

It is alleged that in a number of cases, whatever the gubernatorial overloads hand over to their appointee chairmen, is simply shared among officials and their political godfathers and cronies. Since there is often little or no work to superintend in their local council areas, it is alleged that many Local Council Chairmen have their permanent residence in the state capital or even in Abuja, and they visit their local government areas a couple of times a month to supervise the sharing of the monthly allocations and engage in some public relations enterprise in preparation for the next round of elections or political appointments!

The Disastrous Effects of Corruption

Corruption in Nigeria is indeed systemic. In other words, Corruption is entrenched in the system. And the unwholesome consequences are legion. Corruption has bred inefficiency and diminished productivity in both the public and private sectors of the economy. It has discouraged investment, fuelled capital flight, increased unemployment and inflation, created an acute degree of poverty, brought about a severe decline in the quality of life and life expectancy in Nigeria, and given Nigeria and Nigerians a terribly bad image in the eyes of the international community. Corruption is an affront on human dignity and an assault on the human conscience, apart from being a negation of the Christian and Muslim vocation to promote righteousness in the world.

Nigeria has been through many lean years, years eaten by the locust. The country has truly suffered at the hands of a succession of punitive rulers – military and civilian – who, like mercenaries were only out to steal, to cheat and to destroy. The protracted nightmare caused by this locust invasion in our land seems to have done greater damage to the Nigerian psyche than many immediately realise. One can readily see the economic, political and social dimensions of our nation's distress, but the negative transformation of the Nigerian psyche in the last few decades has been subliminal and silent, but nevertheless progressive and profound. As a people Nigerians seem today to be too weak to hold on to any dreams, too hungry to stand by any principles, and too blind to see beyond the madness of the moment.

As I look at our national firmament, I see the widespread abandonment of the pursuit of excellence and the glorification of mediocrity in practically every area of life. From politics and economy to education and health care, and from the judiciary and law enforcement to the traditional institutions and religion, Nigerians seem to have settled for expediency and mediocrity. In every area of our life, we seem to have made up our minds that the price to be paid for honesty, fidelity, truth, hard work, discipline and diligence are too high. So, we settle for instant gratification, for the short-cut and for the quick fix. We resort to mutual betrayal, calumniation, opportunism and manipulation in the bid to make it at all costs and by any means.

A Jaundiced Religiosity

Religion itself has been thoroughly exploited and manipulated in Nigeria by smart men and women for political or economic gains. A significant dimension of the religious tension in this country today, has not been caused by those who genuinely practice the two religions, but by those who use religion as a platform for political ascendancy or economic gain.

Christianity in Nigeria today has been turned into a business with few ethical norms, where populism and charlatanism are the order of the day in the founding and running of churches, and where greed and avarice rather than doctrinal differentiation are responsible for the daily emergence of new churches.

True, as I consider the embarrassing disconnect between buoyant religiosity and booming corruption in our land, I think of the Seven Deadly Social Sins identified by Mahatma Gandhi: He lists them as "Politics without principle; pleasure without conscience; wealth without work; commerce without morality; education without character; science without humanity; and worship without sacrifice." Popular religion in Nigeria today, which lacks the essential component of a critical social conscience - as evidenced in the widespread corruption and social decay all over the land – has inadvertently supported the monumental pillars of corruption in the country that have brought so much misery and pain upon the people.

It is true that the individual and social morality of a people are often determined by their religious beliefs and values. All true religions share in common transcendental values and elementary moral principles by which good is sought and evil is avoided. True Christianity promotes very high ethical and moral standards, which if believers try to live by, they will inherit Christ's kingdom of peace. No doubt, these ethical standards that are set before Christians will make for a more just, peaceful and wholesome human society. True Christianity teaches people that the meaning of human life is beyond humanity, and beyond this world, therefore the proper dissemination of the Christian message will help to checkmate the human instinct to grab and to accumulate for self, while neglecting the common good. The preaching of the full message of Christ, which has the cross at its centre, is capable of purging Nigeria of the scourge of corruption. Indeed, the dissemination of authentic Christianity, not the message of convenience that we have become familiar with these days, is capable of transforming Nigeria from the gang of fantastically corrupt nations to the enviable club of the most corruption-free nations of the world!

We Must Defeat this Monster

We have noted that corruption is responsible in large measure for the broken promises, the dashed hopes and the shallow dreams that have characterised the existence of the multitude of Nigerians in the last few years. Corruption can be cited as prominent among the causes of the multiple malaise of our nation. Corruption is a malignant tumour, a cancer that eats its hosts to death. In Nigeria it has brought about too much blood and tears. The struggle against corruption in our national landscape is one for the very survival of the nation itself. The choice before Nigerians is very clear: We either go to war against corruption in all its ramifications with all seriousness, or we shall soon be consumed by this hydra-headed dragon.

Those of us who belong to the adult generation must own up before our young people (who can no longer distinguish right from wrong, and good from evil) that we have betrayed our fatherland and failed to lay the necessary foundation for a prosperous future. We must own up to the fact that we have often stolen food off the hands of our children. Each one of us is guilty to the extent that we have contributed in some way to the mess of the moment directly or indirectly, and as perpetrators and accomplices in various forms of corruption. As parents, teachers, community leaders, politicians, religious leaders and elders, we have often failed to inspire young people to live a life of righteousness. Instead, we have often been a source of scandal to our own children and the children of our country.

Thus, the nation must embark on a programme of rebuilding the individual and collective consciences of its citizens. Leaders of genuine religious bodies must once again see it as their principal role to inculcate the fear of God and the values of honesty, probity, hard work, accountability and concern for the common good in their members. Yet, religious bodies alone cannot do what every segment of the society must do to fight corruption in Nigeria. The generality of Nigerians must pay attention to the provisions of the Criminal Code against the various shades of corruption, especially involving public servants, and insist on the rigorous application of these provisions to all and sundry without fear or favour.

The judicial system must be strengthened, and the law enforcement agencies must be thoroughly cleaned up, re-structured and re-oriented, so that they may become more efficient in detecting and fighting corruption. Without an efficient and disciplined justice system, we cannot hope to have a corruption-free society, no matter how religious the people appear to be. Employers should strive to pay adequate salaries and wages to workers. And finally, the society in general should desist from conferring honours on people whose wealth is questionable. Instead, we must device the means of rewarding genuine efforts in integrity, accountability, honesty and probity. We must find a way of empowering and motivating ordinary Nigerian citizens to raise questions around the moral/character antecedents and especially the source of wealth of aspirants to political office in Nigeria. All Nigerians must be at alert to ensure that their elected representatives operate with truth, honesty and accountability.

A Moral Burden and a Call to Action

As a nation awash with outward religiosity, we are indeed today confronted with a moral burden which must be squarely addressed, and urgently too, for the degenerate system cannot sustain for much longer. We need a wholesale doctoring of our individual and collective consciences to make them more sensitive to the concept of right and wrong and of good and evil. We need a reconstruction of our damaged corporate psyche in order to find our bearing in the global community of the twenty-first century. We need a fundamental re-envisioning that will involve a re-definition of our communal ethos, a re-appreciation of our social habits and a re-prioritization of our national values. Yes, we need an ethical and moral revolution in these climes if all the elements of our national existence that have fallen apart are to be brought together.

Yes, as part of the desired ethical and moral revolution, we need to help our various institutions of state put in place new arrangements that would ensure that the paths to public service are not as smooth and attractive as they are now for rogues, thieves and brigands, and that the gains of office are not as rewarding as they are today for men and women of easy virtue who have no business in leadership, but who are simply gunning for the keys of the national, state or local government treasury. The desired change will come about only when the various stakeholders in the Nigerian society, including religious leaders, staunchly

reject the ignominious status-quo that throws up for leadership positions
men and women of base character and dubious wealth.

Time is running out for the Nigerian leaders and people. With the
widespread disengagement, bitterness and resentment in the land, and
with a violent culture already entrenching itself in several parts of the
country, there are ominous signs in the horizon of an impending popular
revolt, or what is called the revenge of the poor. For indeed as presently
constituted, the superstructure we have in place in Nigeria is only a pack
of cards that will soon come crashing down. But if today the Nigerian
people – including Christian and Muslim politicians – experience the
much-needed conversion and toe the line of sanity and integrity, we may
yet pull back from the brink of disaster. There appears to me to be only
one way out of the mess of the moment: the way of ethical and moral
revolution, for it is better to light a candle than forever curse the
darkness!

Some Strategies for Fighting Corruption

We need a multi-pronged, multi-faceted, multi-sectoral and multi-
dimensional approach to the fight against corruption in Nigeria since the
disease itself comes in many shapes and forms. I humbly propose the
following strategies be introduced, or strengthened if they are already
among the strategies in use:

1. Nigerians must work hard to strengthen democratic structures in the
   country, for our fight against corruption will not succeed under the
   present system that is only one step away from military dictatorship.
   Civil society must be on the alert to ensure that our elected
   representatives operate with the highest standards of accountability and
   stewardship. It is indeed the responsibility of civil society groups to
   constantly drag the feet of those in the corridors of power to the fire of
   democracy.
2. All educated Nigerians should get familiar with the provisions of the
   Criminal Code against the various shades of corruption, especially
   those involving public servants. Civil society groups should ensure that
   these provisions are rigorously applied to all and sundry without fear or
   favour.
3. The judicial system must be strengthened, and the rule of law must be
   entrenched. We cannot make progress with the fight against corruption

as long as there is so much impunity in the land, with many seemingly operating above the law, as the anti-corruption agencies find it extremely difficult to successfully prosecute high profile persons accused of corruption.

4. The law enforcement agencies must be thoroughly cleansed, re-structured, re-orientated and highly motivated to make them more efficient in detecting, investigating and prosecuting cases of corruption. There should be no room in modern Nigeria for barely literate young men to be recruited into the police force. It is time to raise the entry qualification for recruitment into the Nigerian Police Force to first degree graduates. We turn out more than enough graduates each year to take care of this.

5. Employers of labour should be constantly encouraged to pay adequate salaries and wages to workers and make provision for their retirement benefits. Workers should not be paid such slave wage as to make them easily susceptible to temptation. Government and corporate organisations should do more towards making Nigeria a welfare state where basic infrastructures are in place that will make life tolerable for even the least paid workers and their families.

6. Nigerians in general should device the means of rewarding hard work, honesty and integrity, and desist from conferring honours to people whose source of wealth is questionable. The country does not lack good people, but our leadership recruitment system as presently constituted tends to throw up rogues, 419ers and fugitives for public office, for chieftaincy titles and for national honours, while those with true leadership credentials are relegated to the background. Civil society agencies can help to seek out men and women of character with good track records, and encourage them to go into politics, and where necessary, sponsor them financially.

7. The antecedents of those who present themselves for public office must be thoroughly investigated *"to the third and fourth generations!"* Thus, even if a young man has never held public office and never been known to steal or misappropriate public fund, he should still be disqualified from public office if his parents or grandparents are discovered to have looted the treasury of the country, the state or the local government area, or if he is discovered to have evaded legitimate tax, forged any documents, or done anything dishonourable at some point in his life.

8. Civil Society groups need to insist that the declaration of assets by public officers should be a public thing. The present practice of secret declaration of assets is of no use in our fight against corruption.

9. Nigerians who desire to see that a truly accountable democratic governance system takes root in the country, must start thinking of a major reform or otherwise a total dislodgement of the structures of traditional rulership in our society, which are remnants of primitive feudalism. These structures (which we are attempting to operate alongside democracy), are by their very nature and practice undemocratic and sometimes even dictatorial.

10. Next to be dismantled is the "big man syndrome," by which thieves, crooks and looters of the commonwealth are adulated in the society because they are "big men" or children of "big men." The people at the grassroots who are always flocking around these "big men" should be helped to see the cause-and-effect relationship between the corruption and profligacy of these big men and their own ever worsening economic and social fortunes. Civil society groups must work towards dismantling the big man syndrome in the Nigerian society and ensure the equality of all citizens before the law if we must root out executive profligacy and ensure transparency and accountability in the society.

11. The section 308 of the 1999 Constitution which guarantees immunity from prosecution for our President, Vice President, Governors and their Deputies, even on account of criminal charges, must be expunged from our law books, if we are serious about the fight against corruption.

12. We must start calling a spade a spade. Corruption is stealing. Nigerian languages all have words for "stealing," but they often lack adequate expressions for "corruption."

13. Unexamined ethnic loyalty is an obstacle on our way to a truly transparent society with accountable leadership. Right-thinking Nigerian individuals and groups must work hard against that form of ethnic bigotry by which acts of corruption are condoned or tolerated if committed by an individual from one's ethnic group. Corrupt officials have often used the ethnic card when their atrocities are exposed, and in many instances their kith and kin have rallied round to defend them.

14. a. Religious bodies should see it as their principal role to inculcate the fear of God and the values of honesty, probity, hard work, accountability and concern for the common good in their members. Nigerians are notorious for their religiosity, and no religion encourages corruption, so religious leaders must demonstrate to their members that vibrant religiosity and rampant corruption cannot exist side by side.

b. Religious leaders should help identify the many faces of corruption in the society. They should exercise utmost caution in conferring honours on people, because such people automatically become role models for the younger generation.

c. Religious bodies should compose general prayers against bribery and corruption, such as the Prayer Against Bribery and Corruption that the members of the Catholic Church have been saying since September 1998.

d. Religious leaders should challenge their members to take oaths or make pledges publicly (in the Church or in the Mosque, before the worshiping community) against all acts of corruption, in the following or similar words: "God our heavenly father, I thank you for the good things that you have given to Nigeria for the good of all. I stand (or kneel) before you today to make a personal commitment to fight corruption. I will not ask for and not take a bribe. I will not misuse my position for private or selfish gain. I will not misappropriate public funds. I will not inflate contracts or be a beneficiary of inflated contracts. I will not procure or conspire with others to procure fake documents...."

e. Our new Churches should de-emphasize the prosperity gospel at this time, for the gospel of success and prosperity at this time of distress in our country tends to aggravate, rather than abate corruption, because it often makes people believe that without hard work you can become rich simply by worshipping God correctly, and since the earth and its resources come from God (and I am a child of God), it doesn't seem to matter how the money comes! All right-thinking Christians must challenge this misrepresentation of the Christian message.

Conclusion: Call for a new National Pledge

Let me repeat here what I have advocated elsewhere: that our circumstances in Nigeria call for the formulation and adoption of a new National Pledge or Declaration, even if an interim one, to drive home the painful lessons of the few decades of debauchery, years that were eaten by the locust. I propose that Nigerians recite the following lines daily, until corruption is wiped out of our land:

I pledge my commitment to the emergence of a new Nigeria,
recognising that greed and avarice are a cancer that eats its own host to death,

that corruption ultimately kills not only the victims, but also the perpetrators,
and that unless we change our course we are bound to end up where we are headed.
I pledge my commitment to the emergence of a new Nigeria,
recognising that righteousness exalts a nation,
but that corruption is a reproach to a people,
and that where there is no vision the people soon perish.
So, help me God to renounce these evils in myself,and to fight them in Nigeria with all the resources you have bestowed upon me! Amen.

Postscript: R.I.P.

It is the end of an era for this land
Drenched with the tears of the poor
Let me be part of the funeral of the moment
So, give me the brush and the chisel

I want to celebrate my artistic ingenuity
On billboards and signboards
I want to celebrate in dirge and epitaph
The eclipse of reason on our national landscape

Make me many tombstones
And I would inscribe on them this epitaph
Send me many mourners
And I would lead them in this dirge:

Here lies the ruins of a nation
Of greed and graft" "Behold the remains
Of a land of deceit and mischief

See the stumps of a generation
Of idiots and bigots."
On the wall of every government building or project
Where workers are on strike
I shall paint the face of nemesis
The vindictive guest of the moment.
By the entrance of every school or university
That is closed down
I shall make a graffiti

Of the visitation of retribution
On a land that was reckless in corruption.
At the gate of every teaching hospital or clinic
That is rotting away
I shall plant the intimidating tombstone
Against a generation whose daily life
Was a death wish
I shall remember to add
For the sake of posterity
That "This giant in the sun collapsed
Not due to external attack
But internal decay.
Requiescat in pace!
(From *Fragments of Truth* by Fr. George Ehusani, 1997, page 30).

CHAPTER THIRTY ONE

Role of Religion and Culture in Curbing Corruption

*Presented at a Policy Roundtable by the Savannah Centre for Diplomacy,
Democracy and Development on the Future of the Anti-Corruption
Campaign in Nigeria, Shehu Yar'Adua Centre, Abuja,
February 28 – March 1, 2018.*

Introduction

Although corruption is a relative concept, being a function of specific normative, social, historical, cultural, economic and political circumstances as well as legal instruments, it is generally understood to entail deliberate malpractices that violate due process and are aimed at personal gain or advantage and selfish enrichment, in violation of the law and at the expense of the common good. Corruption covers a broad range of wrongdoings or corrupt practices that are basically unethical and morally reprehensible, ranging from the giving and taking of bribe, to the use of public office for the advancement of purely private interests, and from the misapplication or misappropriation of public funds to outright fraud and embezzlement. What is common to all forms of corruption is that they threaten and, if not checked, destroy the social order and the common good. Corruption has aggravated poverty, fuelled conflict, brought about misery, sustained injustice, and promoted bad governance and underdevelopment. For this reason, corruption is to be seen as a deadly cancer that must be reduced to the barest minimum if it cannot be completely eliminated in the society.

An Anatomy of the Culture of Corruption

Corruption has been described as a *soft state* variable, a soft state being one that is steeped in amoral politics and crippled by serious problems of credibility; one that is generally not able to enforce its will, especially in matters that have ethical and moral considerations. Edward Banfield, in his classic book, *The Moral Basis of a Backward Society*, says that the soft state is the product of a corrupt political culture or what he calls *amoral familism*, in which governance is non-accountable, public office is used for private gain, and persons are placed in high positions of responsibility on account of patronage rather than merit. The Nigerian variants of what Banfield called *amoral familism* include patrimonialism, prebendalism, clientelism, and the "politics of the belly", or what in recent times has come to be known as "stomach infrastructure." This state of affairs is a recipe for chaos, anarchy and doom, and is therefore antithetical to wholesome development.

Corruption has its foundation in certain undesirable cultural practices, in the lack of appreciation of the common good imperative, in certain remnants of primitive feudalism, in the absence of democratic structures that promote accountability and ensure checks and balances, in the culture of impunity and executive lawlessness, in the absence of a sufficient number of nationally recognised and accepted role models in integrity, in the absence of a sense of national cohesion, and finally in the absence of a clearly articulated and programmatically disseminated set of core national values.

A class of commentators would locate some of these problems in our experience with colonialism and the mental, socio-cultural and political distortions that it brought about. The colonial system set the state apart from society, produced pathological social formations, and engendered an endemic legitimacy crisis of the state, whereby there is a widespread sense of alienation (of the people) from the state, and the destruction of the sense of joint ownership of the state by the civic public. That is why in Nigeria, government business is often perceived as nobody's business; government funds, government property or public infrastructure are seen as belonging to "no one," and could therefore be appropriated by "smart" individuals and groups without any qualms of conscience. Such behaviour is often not seen as stealing. Instead, perpetrators of such corrupt practices are often celebrated by their kinsmen and women for being smart, and for having "done well for themselves." They are rewarded with chieftaincy titles by the village monarchs and awarded honorary doctorates by their state Universities. This is the tragedy of the state and the alienated civic public in Nigeria - a colonial legacy that somehow has remained a remote cause of corruption, but which in my view has not been sufficiently interrogated by many individuals and groups that would want to reduce corruption in Nigeria and many other African countries with similar problems.

Secondly, while the traditional African society was governed by the abiding social morality that, amongst others, emphasized the obligations of the individual to the community and expected the individual to be an agent of community development and defender of community interests, the modern civic public in Nigeria seems to be operating in a moral vacuum. It is terrible for a society to operate within a naked public square, a public square devoid of core values, a public square denuded by the absence of role models or leaders of integrity. This is the reality of our country today. This moral vacuum manifests itself in behaviours that would have been considered abominable and reprehensible in the traditional society, but which today are commonplace. Thus the failure to integrate the concept of the common good, which flourished in the traditional society into the modern (post-colonial) civic public, is responsible in part for several manifestations of corruption, including embezzlement, misappropriation, favouritism, and electoral fraud.

The Place of Religion in the fight against Corruption

Religion features at the very beginning of our nation's constitution. In the preamble to the 1999 Nigerian constitution, it is affirmed that we intend to live together as one united country under God. Indeed the overwhelming majority of Nigerians are religious people. We believe in the supremacy of God. We believe that God is the very basis of our individual lives and our corporate existence. We believe in and relate to supernatural realities through prayers and supplications. We find churches, mosques, shrines and sundry prayer houses everywhere in the land. We take part in crusades, worship sessions and vigils; we offer sacrifices and observe fasting days and religious holidays; and we go in large numbers on religious pilgrimages to Jerusalem and Mecca, taking pride in being called Jerusalem Pilgrim (JP) or Alhaji the rest of our lives.

Within this religious firmament, priests, pastors and prophets, as well as sheikhs, imams and gurus of all sorts, are swelling in number and having a field day. In the last few years, a new dimension has also been added to the thriving religious enterprise. It is the increased patronage of high-ranking public officials who not only openly call for and sponsor regular prayer sessions in different prayer houses, but have themselves become religious leaders, and prayer merchants, often appearing at religious events with all the paraphernalia of public office, and sometimes grabbing the microphone to deliver sanctimonious sermons and earth-shaking prayers.

With all our outward display of religiosity, one would have expected to see a very high degree of social morality in Nigeria, since all world religions generally promote truth, justice, honesty and probity, but this is not the case. There is an embarrassing contradiction between the high ethical demands of the two religions which the majority of Nigerians profess, and the phenomenon of corruption, greed and graft that has earned our country an unenviable place among the gang of corrupt nations. Recall the rather unguarded but embarrassingly damning statement of the former British Prime Minister David Cameron to the effect that Nigeria and Afghanistan are the world's most fantastically corrupt countries! Only recently, Transparency International placed Nigeria in the 148th position out of about 180 countries surveyed, in the corruption perceptions index, down from the 136th position we were alleged to have occupied previously.

While such a damning verdict of a Western leader or that of Transparency International may be contested on many grounds by patriotic Nigerians, we cannot run away from the truth that in recent times, corruption has almost attained the status of state policy in Nigeria. Yes, some keen observers of the phenomenon actually say that corruption is so endemic in the Nigerian society that the socio-economic and political system can almost not function without it. Corruption in its many shapes and sizes has continued to flourish in Nigeria - from the petty bribery taken by the clerk in the office or the policeman at the checkpoint, to the grand corruption by which huge project contracts are hurriedly awarded, not for the sake of the common good, but because of the greed of the awarding official, who requires some money via contract "kick-backs."

Fraud, thievery and roguery have been the order of the day, even as our environment is awash with prayers and ritual sacrifices to the God of truth, justice and righteousness. It doesn't seem to be a matter of contradiction for many highly placed Nigerians that they embezzle or misappropriate stupendous amounts of public and company (or even church) funds, while at the same time struggling to occupy the front rows or take religious titles and other honours in their churches and mosques. Examination malpractice is witnessed on a wide scale, from the common entrance examination organised for placement of 10-year-olds into colleges to the final qualifying examination at the Nigerian Law School. It is alleged that unscrupulous parents and criminally minded teachers are not only accomplices, but sometimes initiators of these shameful practices.

Many Nigerians often fraudulently procure medical certificates of fitness from hospitals when they have not undergone any medical tests. They also obtain sick leave permits from doctors, when they are hale and hearty. They sometimes falsify the age of their children and obtain fake birth certificates in order to get them into nursery or primary schools earlier than the stipulated age. Holding the Bible or Quran in court, they vow to tell the truth and nothing but the truth, only to tell a bundle of lies. They routinely swear to false affidavits in order to claim some undeserved benefits and make false age declarations when seeking employment or admission into institutions of learning. Many of those who today hold drivers' licences, have never seen what a V.I.O. or FRSC testing ground looks like. They simply pay for the licence and declare themselves drivers, putting at risk not only their own lives, but also the lives of other road users.

Many Nigerians, including seemingly pious Christians and Muslims, who would go to war in defence of their religions, have no qualms of conscience when they pay to obtain yellow cards without the necessary inoculation for which the card is supposed to be evidence. Many of our countrymen and women who flock to churches on Sunday and fill the mosques on Friday are at one time or the other involved in such fraudulent activities as evading tax, issuing and obtaining of fake receipts, over-invoicing and under-invoicing, importation of fake drugs, petty and large-scale bribery, fake audit reports, "creative book-keeping," "round-tripping," and advance fee fraud. All these practices are so commonplace and so widespread that many young Nigerians are today unable to distinguish between good and evil or between right and wrong.

Corruption is an affront on human dignity and an assault on the human conscience, apart from being a negation of the Christian and Muslim vocation to promote righteousness in the world. Many of our countrymen and women who engage in the sharp practices listed above would like to be seen as good and religious people. But in truth, are they? Do they really know the God of Abraham, Isaac and Jacob, the God of holiness and righteousness, who in Leviticus 19:2 says, "Be holy for I the Lord am holy?" Do they really know the God of Moses and Joshua who on Mount Sinai presented the 10 commandments as the terms of his contract with his people, insisting that fidelity to this ethical code is what will distinguish his people from all others? Do Nigerians who claim to worship God, but who at the same time offer and take bribe, defraud, evade tax and circumvent just laws in numerous ways, do such Nigerians really know the God of Moses who in Exodus 22:8 says, "You will accept no bribes, for a bribe blinds the clear-sighted and is the cause of the ruin of the upright?" Do they know the God of the prophets who in Isaiah 33:15 says that the person who will be qualified to be in his presence is the one who "acts uprightly and speaks honestly, who scorns to get rich by extortion, who rejects bribes out of hand, who refuses to listen to plans involving bloodshed and shuts his eyes rather than countenance crime...?"

Do Nigerian worshippers who make a daily show of their religiosity know that what the Lord truly requires of those who know him is (as we read in Micah 6:8) "to love tenderly, to do justice, and to walk humbly before your God?" While preparing for the coming of Jesus, John the Baptist condemned the kind of religion that thrives side by side with corruption as empty ritualism. In Luke 3:13-14 he told those who had gathered to listen to him, among whom were soldiers and tax collectors: "Exact no more than the appointed rate...No intimidation! No extortion! Be content with your pay!"

Jesus Christ himself denounced the kind of religious practice that was not matched by high moral and ethical standards in private and social life. A comprehensive discussion of these standards can be found in the Sermon on the Mount (Matthew 5-7). They include a high level of truth and honesty in interpersonal and social relationships, a high sense of purity, modesty and humility, a profound sense of self-sacrifice, a readiness to forgive as often as one is offended and a disposition towards peace and non-violence. He made his disciples realise that not all who claim to be his followers (not all who say, Lord, Lord) will enter the kingdom of heaven, but only those who do the will of the Father in heaven. The will of the Father in heaven is that they be perfect as the heavenly Father himself is perfect (Matthew 5:48).

Christianity makes no room for crooks and fraudsters. It has no place for those who offer or receive a bribe. It has no place for those who would lie and cheat. Genuine Christianity cannot accommodate much of what they call "the Nigerian factor" today. It has no place for those who would use ill-gotten wealth to manipulate the political process. Instead, corruption is a negation of the Christian vocation to build here on earth a kingdom of justice, love and peace. Faced therefore with the contradiction and the embarrassment of a booming religiosity in the midst of an environment that stinks with corruption and indiscipline, some critically-minded Christians have come to the conclusion that what is spreading like wildfire in contemporary Nigeria in the name of Christianity, is not genuine Christianity at all, but a mass movement with elements of Christian ritualism, one that is in large measure shallow, hollow, superficial, noisy and devoid of substance and depth. Popular Christianity in contemporary Nigeria is often materialistic and individualistic in orientation, with an incredibly high sense of devotion to the cult of (material and physical) prosperity, success and healing, and with little or no attention at all given to the social morality of the believing persons.

The brand of Christianity that is experiencing the fastest growth in Nigeria today does not seem to have a place for the notion of the cross, suffering and sacrifice, which constitute the centre of traditional Christian doctrine and life. That is why at a time when Nigeria needs religious leaders and groups to spearhead a moral revolution and an ethical re-orientation for a nation and its people that have been brought low by a life of debauchery, we hear little more than prosperity extravaganza and healing bonanza! At a time when Christian leaders and groups should use the message of the Cross and a modest and austere lifestyle to contradict the crass materialism and extreme economic liberalism of our age that are daily crushing the poor, we are confronted with scandalously expensive churches, harbouring disgustingly rich priests and nauseatingly flashy pastors, whose marks of success include palatial mansions, state-of-the-art cars, expensive jewels, and custom-designed suits. This brand of Christianity fuels corruption, encourages indolence, and promotes mental distortion.

Interrogating the Social Values and Cultural Practices that Fuel Corruption

Corruption cannot be fought, let alone defeated in a vacuum. To root out this deadly virus from our national landscape, we must seriously interrogate and, wherever possible, change those degenerate cultural habits and practices, as well as the religious beliefs and abuses that fuel corruption in our society, in addition to strengthening the democratic system, the legal structures, the judicial processes and the regime of sanctions in our society.

Human beings will generally desire, work for, and gravitate towards acquiring those tangible and non-tangible things which society celebrates or places a high premium upon at a particular time in its history. Researchers from a cross-section of disciplines today agree that people are often animated, oriented and motivated by some pictures of the good life that has been presented to them and which captures their imagination. They generally gravitate towards such a picture, putting all their energies into pursuing that goal or that vision of flourishing where they are told happiness and fulfilment are to be found. Societal beliefs and values, therefore, constitute the growing child's pedagogies of desires.

As we seek to root out corruption from our national landscape, we must ask ourselves the following critical questions: What vision of the good life have we succeeded in transmitting to the young people in our society through the various agents of socialisation in Nigeria? In what direction have we fired the imagination of those whom we raise in our homes, and others whom we train in our schools, colleges and vocational centres? Towards which ultimate goals have we inspired, animated, motivated and mentored our people to direct their energies?

From what we see played out in the lives of the majority of our people – so well reflected in leadership conduct and character, what our people have been taught to SEEK after in life, what they WANT at the gut level of their being, is not to live a life of integrity and leave behind a legacy of service and sacrifice for the common good. No, the ultimate quest of many people in our society today is to acquire power, prestige, high status, abundant wealth, social influence, and a legacy of landed property in Nigeria as well as in Europe and America, which they take pride in willing to their children and grandchildren. Thus, the rhythms of life, the cultural patterns, the social framework, or the values celebrated daily in our towns and villages, as well as in the regular and social media, are daily teaching our young people to go for it, to get rich quick, to amass enormous wealth, to build many houses with no thought given to the common good, or consideration for ethics and morals. These are the values that define our social morality, and they are by and large responsible for the all-pervading nature of corruption in our society.

Thus, to stamp out corruption from the Nigerian landscape:

i. The cultural practice whereby Nigerians take pride in leaving landed property for children and grandchildren must be interrogated because it fuels corruption.

ii. The cultural practice whereby Nigerians take pride in marrying many wives and having many children, even when it has become expensive to raise just one or two children, must be interrogated because it fuels corruption.

iii. The cultural practice whereby privileged Nigerians enjoy being surrounded by a retinue of personal aides and servants, numerous security agents and hangers-on (like primitive feudal lords), and driving around in lengthy motorcades, must be interrogated because it fuels corruption.

iv. The cultural practice whereby Nigerians take pride in celebrating expensive weddings, birthdays and funerals must be interrogated because it fuels corruption.

v. The cultural practice whereby Nigerians honour and adulate rich persons – giving them chieftaincy titles and awarding them honorary doctorate degrees, with no one caring to ask how such individuals made their money, must be interrogated because it fuels corruption.

vi. The cultural practice whereby the common good is often neglected completely while we promote individual and group good must be interrogated because it fuels corruption. This poor sense of the common good makes many Nigerians think that public property is no one's property. It is for the same reason that Nigerians say of someone who only worked in the public service but who has amassed a lot of ill-gotten wealth, that such a person "has done well for himself."

In place of the widespread disposition to primitive acquisition in contemporary Nigerian culture, we should start working towards bringing our young people up to desire to leave behind a legacy of hard work, humility, integrity, simplicity, a high sense of patriotism, courage, service, sacrifice and commitment to the common good.

Interrogating the Pop Religion that is Devoid of Social Morality in Nigeria

Nigerians make a lot of noise in the name of religion, but their lives often betray a near-total lack of the sense of the fear of God, the sense of right and wrong, the strong desire for and commitment to the virtuous life and hatred for sin, commitment to the common good, care and concern for the poor, discipline or self-control, self-sacrifice, chastity, modesty, frugality and the aversion to violence that are traditionally associated with truly religious people. It does not matter whether it is Christianity or Islam, Buddhism or Hinduism; religiosity used to be closely associated with the practice of virtue and the cultivation and promotion of a life of discipline, frugality and self-abnegation. It is incredible how, in this country, we have found a way of practising and promoting a kind of pop religion that is devoid of the above critical elements of true, authentic religiosity. No wonder the widespread rot in the land.

The ethical and moral teachings of our various religions, however, remain intact and could be found in the Hebrew and Christian Bible and the Muslim Qur'an and *Hadith*. It is not difficult to see that the practical lives of many so-called religious people in this society run contrary to the best teachings of their professed religions. No one doubts, for example, that the high ethical standards and strict moral teachings of Jesus Christ and his early disciples as contained in the books of the New Testament will bring about a just and peaceful society if we could only imbibe these teachings and live by them. But to what extent are these high ethical standards and strict moral teachings being adequately taught and accepted by Nigerians who claim to be religious today?

A major part of the challenge before us is how to rid our society of charlatans and con artists who parade themselves as religious leaders and preachers. These people are propagating primitive superstition rather than liberating the people from the shadows of a by-gone pre-scientific era of witches and wizards and evil spirits and demons. Instead of teaching the people the way of discipline, honesty, truth and justice, they are promoting corruption in the land by denying, for example, the cause-and-effect relationship in the order of nature between hard work and prosperity.

Indeed, popular religion in Nigeria today, which lacks the essential component of a critical social conscience - as evidenced in the widespread corruption and social decay all over the land – has inadvertently supported the monumental pillars of corruption in the country that have brought so much misery and pain upon the people. Yet, it is true that the individual and social morality of a people are often determined by their religious beliefs and values. All true religions share in common such transcendental values, and elementary moral principles by which good is sought and evil is avoided. Authentic Christianity promotes very high ethical and moral standards. No doubt, these ethical standards that are set before Christians will make for a more just, peaceful and wholesome human society.

Authentic Christianity, for example, teaches people that the meaning of human life is beyond humanity, and beyond this world. Therefore, the proper dissemination of the Christian message will help checkmate the human instinct to grab and accumulate for self while neglecting the common good. The preaching of the entire message of Christ, which has the Cross at its centre, is capable of purging Nigeria of the scourge of corruption. Indeed, the dissemination of authentic Christianity, not the message of convenience known as the prosperity gospel that we have become familiar with these days, can transform Nigeria from the gang of fantastically corrupt nations to the enviable club of the most corruption-free nations of the world!

Acknowledging our Collective Responsibility

Those of us who belong to the adult generation must own up before our young people (who can no longer distinguish right from wrong, and good from evil) that we have betrayed our fatherland and failed to lay the necessary foundation for a prosperous future. We must own up to the fact that we have often stolen food from the hands of our children. Each one of us is guilty to the extent that we have contributed in some way to the mess of the moment directly or indirectly, as perpetrators and accomplices in various forms of corruption. As parents, teachers, community leaders, politicians, religious leaders and elders, we have often failed to inspire young people to live a life of righteousness. Instead, we have often been a source of scandal to our own children and the children of our country.

Call to Action

As a nation awash with outward religiosity, we are indeed today confronted with a moral burden which must be squarely addressed, and urgently too, for the degenerate system cannot sustain for much longer. We need a wholesale doctoring of our individual and collective consciences to make them more sensitive to the concept of right and wrong and of good and evil. We need a reconstruction of our damaged corporate psyche in order to find our bearing in the global community of the twenty-first century. We need a fundamental re-envisioning that will involve a re-definition of our communal ethos, a re-appreciation of our social habits and a re-prioritization of our national values. Yes, we need an ethical and moral revolution in these climes if all the elements of our national existence that have fallen apart are to be brought together.

Yes, as part of the desired ethical and moral revolution, we need to help our various institutions of state put in place new arrangements that would ensure that the paths to public service are not as smooth and attractive as they are now for rogues, thieves and brigands, and that the gains of office are not as rewarding as they are today for men and women of easy virtue who have no business in leadership, but who are simply gunning for the keys of the national, state or local government treasury. The desired change will come about only when the various stakeholders in the Nigerian society, including religious leaders, staunchly reject the ignominious status-quo that throws up for leadership positions men and women of base character and dubious wealth.

Time is running out for Nigerian leaders and people. With the widespread disengagement, bitterness and resentment in the land, and with a violent culture already entrenching itself in several parts of the country, there are ominous signs on the horizon of an impending popular revolt, or what is called the revenge of the poor. For indeed, as presently constituted, the superstructure we have in place in Nigeria is only a pack of cards that will soon come crashing down. But if today the Nigerian people – including Christian and Muslim politicians, experience the much-needed conversion and toe the line of sanity and integrity, we may yet pull back from the brink of disaster. There appears to me to be only one way out of the mess of the moment: the way of ethical and moral revolution, for it is better to light a candle than forever curse the darkness!

At this point, I would like to outline the following strategies that I believe will help in curbing corruption in our society:

1. Nigerians, in general, should devise the means of rewarding hard work, honesty and probity and desist from conferring honours on people whose wealth is questionable. The country does not lack good people, but the system we are operating today is such that it throws up rogues, 419ers and fugitives for public office, for chieftaincy titles and for national honours. Civil society agencies can help to seek out men and women of character with good track records, and encourage them to

go into politics, or even help sponsor them financially.

2. The antecedents of those who present themselves for public office must be thoroughly investigated "to the third and fourth generations!" Thus even if a young man has never held public office and never been known to steal or misappropriate public fund, he should still be disqualified from public office if his parents or grandparents are discovered to have amassed wealth illegally, or if he is discovered to have evaded legitimate tax, forged any documents, or done anything dishonourable at some point in his life.

3. Civil Society groups need to insist that the declaration of assets by public officers should be a public thing. The present practice of secret declaration of assets is of no use in our fight against corruption.

4. The feudal structures that we still have in place all over this country (based as they are on the notion of inequality) will not help our fight against corruption. For example, the concept of "ka bi o osi" in Yoruba culture and tradition cannot survive simultaneously with accountable democratic governance, to the extent that the "King" by his very title, cannot be held to account by anyone. Groups committed to the equality of all persons under the law should consider mounting a campaign for the dislodgement of the "Kabiyesi" syndrome.

5. Next to be dismantled is the "big man syndrome," by which thieves, crooks and looters of the commonwealth are adulated in the society because they are "big men" or children of "big men." The people at the grassroots who are always flocking around these "big men" should be helped to see the cause-and-effect relationship between the corruption and profligacy of these big men and their own ever-worsening economic and social fortunes. Civil society groups must work towards dismantling the big man syndrome in the Nigerian society and ensure equality of all citizens before the law if we must root out executive profligacy and ensure transparency and accountability in the society.

6. With our history of endemic corruption in high places, Nigerians must now consider if section 308 of the 1999 Constitution which guarantees immunity from prosecution for our President, Vice-President, Governors and their Deputies, even on account of criminal charges, should not be expunged from our law books.

7. We must start calling a spade a spade. Corruption is stealing. Nigerian languages all have words for "stealing," but they often lack adequate expressions for "corruption."

8. Ethnic bigotry or unexamined ethnic loyalty is an obstacle on our way to a truly transparent society with accountable leadership. Right-

thinking Nigerian individuals and groups must work hard against that form of ethnic bigotry by which acts of corruption are condoned or tolerated if committed by an individual from one's ethnic group. Corrupt officials have often used the ethnic card when their atrocities are exposed, and in many instances, their kith and kin have rallied round to defend them.

9.

a. Religious bodies should see it as their principal role to inculcate the fear of God and the values of honesty, probity, hard work, accountability and concern for the common good in their members. Nigerians are notorious for their religiosity, and no religion encourages corruption, so religious leaders must demonstrate to their members that vibrant religiosity and rampant corruption cannot exist side by side.

b. Religious leaders should help identify the many faces of corruption in the society. They should exercise utmost caution in conferring honours on people because such people automatically become role models for the younger generation.

c. Religious bodies should think of composing general prayers against bribery and corruption, such as the Prayer Against Bribery and Corruption that the members of the Catholic Church have been saying since 1998.

d. Religious leaders should challenge their members who get elected or appointed to leadership positions, to take oaths or make pledges publicly (in the Church or in the Mosque, before the worshipping community) against all acts of corruption, in the following or similar words: *"God our heavenly Father, I thank you for the good things that you have given to Nigeria for the good of all. I stand (or kneel) before you today to make a personal commitment to fight corruption. I will not ask for or take a bribe. I will not misuse my position for private or selfish gain. I will not misappropriate public funds. I will not inflate contracts or be a beneficiary of inflated contracts. I will not procure or conspire with others to procure fake documents...."*

e. Our new Churches should de-emphasize the prosperity gospel at this time, for the gospel of success and prosperity at this time of distress in our country tends to aggravate, rather than abate corruption, because it often makes people believe that without hard work, you can become rich simply by worshipping God correctly, and it doesn't seem to matter how the money comes! All right-thinking Christians must challenge this misrepresentation of the Christian message.

Conclusion: Need for a New National Pledge!

Finally, our circumstances in Nigeria call for the formulation and adoption of a new National Pledge, to drive home the painful lessons of the years of debauchery, years eaten away by the locusts of corruption. I propose that Nigerians in public and private life recite the following or similar lines daily, until corruption is totally wiped out of the surface of our land:

1. I pledge my commitment to the emergence of a new Nigeria, recognising that corruption is a cancer that eats its own host to death; that corruption ultimately kills not only the victims, but also the perpetrators; and that unless we change our course, we are bound to end up where we are headed.
2. I pledge my commitment to the emergence of a new Nigeria, recognising that thievery, robbery and roguery, by whatever name else it is called, when it becomes king in a land, that land rots; and that when hooliganism and banditry get into high places, the superstructure soon comes crashing down.
3. I pledge my commitment to the emergence of a new Nigeria, recognising that where lawlessness becomes the norm, and illegality becomes the rule, the nation collapses.
4. I pledge my commitment to the emergence of a new Nigeria, recognising that righteousness exalts a nation, but that sin is a reproach to a people; and that where there is no vision, the people soon perish.
   So help me, God, to resist these evils in myself, and to fight them in Nigeria with all the resources you have bestowed upon me!

Index

www.ingramcontent.com/pod-product-compliance
Lightning Source LLC
Chambersburg PA
CBHW061729270326

41928CB00011B/2173